Reading in Primary Schools

Reading in Primary Schools

by Geoffrey R. Roberts
Lecturer in Education
University of Manchester

LONDON
ROUTLEDGE & KEGAN PAUL
NEW YORK : HUMANITIES PRESS

First published 1969
by Routledge & Kegan Paul Ltd
Broadway House, 68-74 Carter Lane
London, E.C.4

Reprinted 1970

Printed in Great Britain
by Northumberland Press Limited
Gateshead

© Geoffrey R. Roberts 1969

ISBN 0 7100 6518 3 (c)
ISBN 0 7100 6519 1 (p)

THE STUDENTS LIBRARY OF EDUCATION has been designed to meet the needs of students of Education at Colleges of Education and at University Institutes and Departments. It will also be valuable for practising teachers and educationists. The series takes full account of the latest developments in teacher-training and of new methods and approaches in education. Separate volumes will provide authoritative and up-to-date accounts of the topics within the major fields of sociology, philosophy and history of education, educational psychology, and method. Care has been taken that specialist topics are treated lucidly and usefully for the non-specialist reader. Altogether, the Students' Library of Education will provide a comprehensive introduction and guide to anyone concerned with the study of education, and with educational theory and practice.

J. W. TIBBLE

Learning to read and the teaching of reading have for long been surrounded with controversy. There have been some new developments in most decades of this century, mostly springing from the impact of the currently favoured psychological theories of learning and behaviour. Young teachers are at times apt to be bemused by the choices open to them in this field, until they find a viewpoint which leads to practices in accord with their own personal skills and styles. In the event it may well be that the existence of a variety of approaches to reading is of fundamental value and every old problem benefits from being seen in a fresh perspective.

This book by Mr Roberts is not the only volume on reading which will be published in the Students' Library. It will be followed by *Children Learning to Read* by Mrs Goodacre. These two books will exemplify two quite different approaches to the study of reading, approaches which will no doubt appeal to somewhat different audiences and which may well be appropriate to rather different circumstances and problems.

Mr Roberts' book on reading should be of great value for teachers looking for an up-to-date psychological point of view in this field. It may well also stir older practitioners sufficiently to make them question in a constructive way their own beliefs and practices, and also the implications of the point of view Mr Roberts has adopted. The notion, for example, that, amongst other things, 'reading is skilled behaviour' is one which may well set off beneficial controversies. Also his approach to reading via the structure of the learning tasks, i.e. by way of linguistic theory as against an approach in terms of the task's relationships to children's learning characteristics, revives in a stimulating form an unresolved issue which has a long history in educational theory. Quite apart however from its general orientation, teachers will find Mr Roberts' book an extremely useful guide to an important and still very active field for research and for practical innovation.

BEN MORRIS

Contents

1
Introduction

Most of the books that have been written about reading
and learning to read have not attempted to describe the
complex skill of reading as a unified operation. A few
books, Stott's and Diack's in particular, have attempted
to explain what happens when reading takes place, and
to draw from this some conclusions about suitable
methods of teaching. The main purpose of this book is to
re-examine reading and learning to read and their relationship with spoken language, and, out of this study, to
attempt to define more clearly the field in which the
teacher has to operate when teaching children to read.
But there is another purpose of this book: it is to consider
the whole range of learning to read for all children in the
primary years, up to the age of eleven.

Many people have assumed that once children could
read simple prose the task of teaching them to read was
finished. Every teacher knows that this is not so, but
only a few do anything significant about it. Children are
left to their own devices, to stumble as best they can into
more efficient reading during the junior school years, and
very little is done to help them. We have been reminded
of this unsatisfactory state of affairs by Dr Joyce Morris.
Yet children's reading in the junior schools has not been
totally neglected. There are many ways in which these

children have been helped to improve their reading. The main trouble has been that these ways were frequently too haphazard in their application and did not achieve the desired standards of efficient reading. It is hoped that this book will stimulate further discussion and result in steps being taken to give all junior school children a skilfully prepared programme, which will improve their ability to use their reading skill as an efficient tool for further learning and enjoyment.

The whole content of the book is an attempt to introduce a greater degree of rigour into the teaching of reading. Whenever this is attempted there is a tendency for the more progressive teachers to fear a return to the formality which bedevilled learning in the infant and junior schools until the advent of the more enlightened approaches of recent years. This fear is misplaced as far as this book is concerned. It is not the intention to advocate a return to an older and discredited approach. It is an attempt to see what can be done to help the child, so that he will progress with the greater ease. Indeed, it is hoped that by differentiating in the mind of the teacher the various skills and sub-skills involved in learning to read, it will be possible in practice to integrate the teaching of reading more precisely and more naturally within the wider objectives of the enlightened primary school. If this can be done, then the child will find learning to read a much easier and engrossing task, and he will be better equipped to participate fully in all the exciting activities that are available.

Whilst accepting the fact that greater informality in the classroom has brought great improvements to the education of primary school children, it has, nevertheless, had undesirable effects in some instances. Undoubtedly, the better teachers can use an informal situation to great advantage, but the less able teacher has sometimes been able to masquerade as a progressive teacher, when in fact the children in the class are learning little or nothing. This is something that is very difficult to eradicate. It is no use laying down an exact programme of what should be done, because teachers and classes differ in so many ways. Therefore the only course left is to attempt to examine in great detail what the child needs to do in order to read a text, and then to consider some of the ways in which the child can be helped. If a teacher is prepared to do this, then she is bound to improve her teaching techniques. Her increased awareness of the implications of her actions and her greater understanding of the processes involved in learning to read will enable her to modify her teaching. This will bring both greater depth and greater flexibility to her teaching, and the child will benefit as a result.

2
Skilled reading

It is very important, in any discussion of ways in which children learn to read and of the teaching that is necessary for rapid progress, to have a clear knowledge of what is involved in the actual process of reading. Bartlett's (1947) approach to the study of skill was to observe first the behaviour in its final form. There seems to be every reason for following his example and to apply this approach to the study of reading and learning to read. If we know what happens when a person reads with skill, then we shall have a clearer notion of how to achieve this desired skill.

TWO MISCONCEPTIONS

However, before examining skilled reading it is necessary to clarify two points which have caused confusion and have led to inaccurate conclusions about the best way to teach reading.

Recognition of words

The first point concerns the statement frequently made that skilled readers recognize words as wholes, implying that they do not have to examine the word letter by letter.

This is so in the case of familiar words, but although skilled readers recognize familiar words at a glance, they recognize unusual or unfamiliar words in a different way. For example, most adults would recognize *gentleman, ladies,* and *stop* at a glance, but most adults would not recognize *geomorphology, ichthyoid, idiosyncratic,* and *hugeous* at a glance. They would have to take a little time to examine the parts of these words and read off the signals, or information, given by the letters of the word : in some cases individual letters and in some cases strings of letters. Outline shape and length, ascenders and descenders, have little to do with recognition of these unfamiliar words. It is the sounds which can be attached to letters or to strings of letters that indicate what the word sounds like. In the case of familiar words, instant recognition is made possible by means of reduced cues : that is, certain features within the word are noted and the skilled reader's knowledge of written language is such that he can make certain assumptions about the remaining features. For example, we can recognize a person who is well-known to us by the cut of his hair and the shape of his fore-head, even though the rest of the face is partly obscured (Neisser, 1964); we can distinguish between the rear ends of two different cars even though we can see only a quarter of each car.

The same applies, of course, to the recognition of strings of words, such as *once upon a time, good morning, needless to say*. When the reader is sufficiently familiar with these strings of words he no longer needs to read off all the signals given by each part of each word.

Later it will be shown that this argument is relevant in the case of young children and, as a consequence, look-and-say should be regarded as a part of the preparatory approach which should be clearly differentiated from word identification and learning to read in the true sense of these phrases. Indeed, where look-and-say persists beyond the necessary preparatory period the children will learn to read by other means, in that they will learn to make correspondences between letters and sounds for themselves. Later, when they have learned the fundamental skills of reading, then look-and-say techniques can be used to achieve a quicker easier rate of reading.

Processing the perceptual input

The second point of possible confusion concerns what is loosely termed perception. It is frequently assumed that seeing the letters of a word, or the words of a sentence, is all that is involved in word recognition. This is an oversimplification. The facts are that in reading the reader sees shapes and he proceeds to interpret these shapes by giving them some auditory significance, so that what has actually happened is something more than merely seeing or perceiving. The reader has associated something from his previous experience—in this case letter sounds—with the abstract letter shapes before him. Hence, to think of letter, word, phrase or sentence recognition as a single act of perception is misleading. A process more accurately described as apperception has taken place, in which the various parts or cues were interpreted; and, like all acts of interpretation, the responses to cues are in some measure subjective.

For example, the word *tlp* would be recognized by a reader. It is the dot above the vertical line and its relationship with *t* and *p* rather than its exact height which helps recognition of the *i*. What is seen is interpreted and the result is the word *tip*. This is how children manage to

6

read their own irregular writing. Backward children frequently have to use this processing procedure when reading what they have written!

This is merely another way of stating that interpretation of perceptual input is distinct from the perception itself. What is seen is interpreted in such a way that it complies with the constraints or rules of language. There is no such word as *tlp*, but there is a word *tip*.

To carry this point a bit further: if the sentence *I should love to see Paris in the the Spring* was placed in a meaningful paragraph and the reader asked to read the passage as quickly as possible, it is doubtful whether he would notice the repetition of the word *the* even though we can reasonably assume that he has seen *the the*. The reader is using his knowledge of language to interpret what he sees.

In a similar way, this process, involving apperception, also occurs when a person reads a passage and interprets the meaning of several sentences. This can be discovered by quickly reading aloud once the following passage and attempting to reproduce what has been read:

As we have already reported, after the rioting of the past weeks, the atmosphere in Hong Kong is now more relaxed in spite of the continued discovery of home-made bombs. Four such bombs were found today and were detonated by police experts.

It is a fair assumption that, although the reader could not reproduce the exact wording and syntax of the passage, he could reproduce the sense.

This has a very important implication. It means that strings of words are retained in the immediate memory store until their sense is revealed. Then the sense is stored so that the immediate memory store is cleared and the reader can take in the next string of words. Some strings, e.g. *As we have already reported*, may be rejected because they contribute little to the meaning of the passage. It follows from this that the texts of children's reading books must consist of connected prose, the meaning of which develops in a sequential manner so that children can extract and retain the sense of the text without having to remember all the individual words. If the texts are not constructed in this manner, and the child has to read a series of statements only loosely connected with each other, the burden on his memory would be too great: too many separate entities would have to be remembered without developing into any form of connected sense.

One of the finest examples of a story which develops and yet employs severe semantic constraints is 'Bullawong' by Jenny Taylor and Terry Ingleby (*My Yellow Book*) and reproduced in the Young Puffin, *Time for a Story* edited by E. Colwell. It is a useful and revealing exercise to compare this story with the stories in such popular reading sets as the Key Words, Happy Venture, and Janet and John Series.

SKILLED READING

Having clarified two points of confusion, it is now possible to consider the process of reading as a whole, beginning with skilled reading.

There are three major factors that should have a profound effect upon the approach to the teaching of reading that is adopted.

Reading is skilled behaviour

The first of these is that reading is skilled behaviour performed in order to obtain information of one kind or another. It can occur at five levels at least—the paragraph, the sentence, the word, the letter string and the letter—and the type of information obtained depends upon the level. Letters convey information about sounds, and this leads on to words, which convey information contributing to meaning, and so on. Therefore, although a reader begins a passage uncertain of any of the information it contains, he reduces this uncertainty, level by level, as he proceeds. The position and order of letters, the juxtaposition of words, the formation of the phrases and the sentences, and the part they play within the paragraph or story—these cover the phonic, syntactic and semantic aspects of language; it is the task of the reader to interpret them in a way which brings meaning to the text. All this is part of the processing of the perceptual input and it emphasizes the importance of a text that flows and develops.

Reading is a linguistic process

The second major factor is that reading is a linguistic process and as such reflects the constraints of language. That is, there is an imposed order at all levels. For example, there are constraints on the consonants which could follow an initial *t*: *h*, *r*, *w*, (and *s* if we include the word *tsetse*). There are constraints on the word that could follow *constraints* at the beginning of this sentence. It could be only one of a very limited number of words. There are constraints on the meaning of the phrase which could follow the opening phrase, *I went to the shops* . . . the more so if this sentence is to be part of a wider passage.

This means that, by familiarity with the constraints of language, the reader can anticipate within certain clearly

9

defined limits what is likely to follow at any of the five levels that I have mentioned. Without this order or constraint reading would be impossible.

It is the reader's task to learn to interpret these constraints in terms of the printed text, and to do so he must have experience in manipulating letters within words, words within strings of words or sentences, sentences within paragraphs or stories. A good example of the way in which letters and sounds can be manipulated within words is illustrated by Dr Gattegno in his demonstration of the use of word charts in the film, 'Words in Colour'. Here it is possible to see a very able teacher teaching children how to manipulate letters and their sounds and in the process interpret them.

Reading and the critical units of language

The final factor concerning skilled reading that should be mentioned is connected with word identification, and it is really a continuation of the last point. In the past there have been several assumptions made about the critical unit of language for the reading process. First the letter was regarded as the proper unit, so the alphabetic method developed; this was followed by the sound of individual letters being considered as the proper unit, so there emerged the early phonic methods; later, the word was regarded by many as the proper unit and the word method or look-and-say became popular; and finally, out of all this, there has begun to evolve a far more sophisticated approach which recognizes the unity of the word but realizes the functions of the letter-sound relationships which constitute each word. Daniels and Diack began this trend and many are beginning to follow.

But we have not yet achieved, by any means, a full working knowledge of how the complete skill of reading is acquired. Recent investigations by Eleanor Gibson and her colleagues indicate that the principal factor in the identification of words is provided by the constraints on letter sequences. They suggest that the critical unit of language in the reading process is not the letter or individual sounds, neither is it the word, but that such a unit is 'the letter group which has an invariant relationship with a phonemic pattern' (Gibson *et al.*, 1962). For example, in the monosyllabic word *pleats*, the child, in order to read well, must learn that the basic readily usable units are the initial-consonant spelling *pl*, the vowel-spelling *ea*, and the final-consonant spelling *ts*. Either some way must be found of telling the child this or he must find it out for himself. Many children are expected to fuse the two sounds, /p/ and /l/, by saying them separately and arriving at the blend /pl/, but this is virtually impossible, as the reader can ascertain. It would be more effective to teach the child the three sounds separately: /p/, /l/, and /p,l/.

Reading is now seen as decoding the phonemic or sound patterns of spoken language rather than decoding single letters. Gibson and her colleagues wisely suggest that these letter/sound correspondences should be introduced in different contexts, so that the child can see them operating in many different words, and thereby learn and understand their invariant relationship. In this way the child will achieve more easily what he has to learn anyhow—to perceive as units the clusters of letters that represent the basic sounds of spoken language. For example, when the child first meets the consonant cluster, *pl*, in his reading book, the teacher should help him with the word in which the cluster appears and should, at the same time, introduce other words containing *pl*, so that the child can see that whatever other letters appear in the word with *pl*, the sound to be attached to that cluster remains the same.

Gibson et al. in some later research (1963) emphasize that it is within words that these units of sound can be predicted by the reader: they should not be presented to the child as meaningless sounds isolated from words. Second, she tentatively suggests that as reading skill improves, the units employed by the reader increase in span, which is the same process as was described earlier in this chapter when mention was made of the skilled reader's recognition of familiar words.

The implications for teachers of Gibson's work will not have been missed, but it may be useful to emphasize them. There should be a greater emphasis on speech and the various types of sounds that contribute to spoken language. Every teacher of children who are about to begin to learn to read should begin with the assumption that the children will not necessarily be aware of the sounds that they are using when they speak. Spoken language has become so automatic, even to the four- and five-year-olds, that they can communicate without having to search consciously for the sounds which form part of their speech. The teacher's task is to help the children to re-examine spoken language. First they must be shown that their speech consists of separate words. This will not be an easy task and it will take some time to accomplish. Formal instruction will merely confuse the young children, so the task will have to be achieved through the individual child's active participation in the dissection and construction of his own language. For example, the following sequence

12

could lead to the extraction of the words *play* and *house* from the child's speech:

Child: I want to play.
Teacher: What do you want?
Child: To play.
Teacher: What do you want to play?
Child: I want to play house.
Teacher: Come to the Wendy House.

If the teacher then writes the two words *play* and *house* for the child, she will then have begun the process of isolating words in both oral and written forms, however hazy this may be to the child at first.

Later the child must learn that words contain sounds of varying numbers, depending upon the word chosen. The teacher can begin with I-spy games involving the initial sounds of words, followed by the final sounds, and eventually involving sounds in the middle of the word. Single letter sounds will be used at first, but as the children grasp the idea, blends and digraphs can be introduced.

Gradually, as the oral sounds are associated with the written letters, whether multiple sounds—morphemes— in the case of words, or single sounds—phonemes—in the case of letters and digraphs, the children begin to participate in manipulative games and exercises. Letters cut out of wood, individual letters printed on small squares of card, strings of letters and small words can provide innumerable opportunities for the child to relate his study of speech and sound to the visual representation of language that is writing. Such work involves not only seeing but manipulating and processing. It will consist mainly of copying words and sentences presented by the teacher in the early stages, but the child will gradually assume the initiative and construct his own sentences and words as he learns to read.

The general conclusions that can be drawn from this brief analysis of skilled reading are twofold. The child must become familiar with a visual system of constraints, just as at an earlier age when, learning to talk, he became familiar with an auditory system of constraints. He must gain a sense of what letter and word combinations are possible and what are not. Second, it is obviously impossible to learn to read without building up a facility for interpreting perceptual input. This processing has to be done at all levels—letter, letter-string, word, sentence, paragraph. But this cannot be done without acquiring a number of sub-skills and, through practice, making these sub-skills automatic. In fact, a skill must be learnt as a basis for an activity.

3
Learning to read

One of the earliest skills a child must learn, when starting
to learn to read, is to recognize that the different letters
vary in shape and that the shape of each letter is invariable. This can be achieved in a variety of ways—alphabet
books, playing with wooden letters, matching individual
letters, tracing with the forefinger letters made of glue
and sand—much of it incidental and unstressed as a part
of learning to read. This can be as much fun as count-
ing and chanting, rhyming and sing-song. However, there
should be as little vocalization of the individual letters as
possible. Any vocalization that does take place should be
within the context of a meaningful word or closely associated with a familiar word.

The sub-skills of reading

The other sub-skills are enumerated below. The order in
which they are acquired by the child does not necessarily
follow exactly the listed order. Naturally, the teaching
method will influence the order, although it cannot alter
it radically because many of the later sub-skills depend on
the acquisition of the earlier ones.

The child must learn, in one way or another the
following:

1. That the printed text tells a story or gives information, i.e. that the visual symbols convey a language message.

2. That the various shapes of letters and words are cues to the various sounds we make when speaking, although the child need not be able to identify specific letters or words at this stage.

3. That there is an *exact* correspondence between the order of sounds spoken and the left to right sequence of *words* as printed—with the spaces between printed words corresponding to (possible) minimal pauses in speech: ə, kæt, sæt, ɔn, ə, mæt = *a cat sat on a mat*.

4. To differentiate visually between the letter shapes: *i* and *p*, *t* and *m*, *b* and *d*, and so on, to include all the letters.

5. To identify letter shapes by their sound: $c = /k/$, $a = /æ/$, $t = /t/$.

6. That there is an *approximate* correspondence between the left-to-right sequence of the *letters* as written and the temporal sequence of phonemes (sounds which make up the word). $c \to a \to t = /k/ \to /æ/ \to /t/$.

7. To differentiate visually between the digraphs (*ea*, *ai*, *ch*, *sh*, *ie*, etc.).

8. To identify the digraphs by their sound: they must learn the various alternatives, e.g. *ea* in *beat*, *idea*, *beautiful*, *ocean*, *great*.

9. To form a meaningful word by synthesizing, in their correct order, meaningless vocal syllables: /ai/, /den/, /tiː/, /fai/ = /aidentiːfai/, (*identify*).

10. To differentiate frequent letter strings, e.g. *-tion*, *str-*, *spr-*, *-ing*, *un-*, etc.

11. To identify these letter strings by their sound: *-tion* = /ʃən/; *-ing* = /iŋ/.

16

12. A variety of strategies for forming and recognizing unfamiliar polysyllabic words.

13. To respond with increasing facility to all the demands made in strategies 1 to 12 so that the whole process becomes more and more automatic, effortless and fluent.

The first three items in this list form the foundation upon which reading ability can most effectively develop, for unless special steps are taken to ensure that the child has some idea of the nature of the task, then he will be perplexed and have no clear idea of what is expected of him. J. F. Reid (1966) illustrated some aspects of this problem in an interesting piece of research reported in the journal of the National Foundation for Research in Education.

There are many ways through which the child can gain an appreciation of the nature of print. For instance, the primary significance of the practice of writing a word or a sentence under a child's drawing is that it emphasizes the symbolic nature of writing and the relevance of order. The child can see the words being written and hear the words being said, and he will realize eventually that there is an exact correspondence between the sequence of the words printed and the order of the words spoken. Similarly, occasionally following the print with the forefinger when reading to a child helps to orientate the child. Another way of introducing a child to order and sequence is by the construction of sentences from words printed on separate pieces of card. And, of course, several other ways could be evolved. Thought and time given to ways in which a child can be introduced to the nature of the task of learning to read would be very fruitful in terms of a more rapid progress when the child enters the more formal stages of learning to read. Understanding cannot be achieved by direct instruction, only through purposeful experience over a period of time. Eventually the initiation of a look-and-say method of 'reading' words and phrases will be part of that experience and, thereby, will partly fulfil item 3.

Learning to read as it is more generally understood begins at items 4, 5 and 6. Not only must these processes be learnt, they must be automatized as quickly as possible, so that the child will be able to execute them with increasing rapidity. It is a laborious task to have to differentiate each letter shape in a word, identify it by its sound, and then try to place the sounds in a sequence when one is uncertain of each of these three processes. Only by increasing familiarity with them does the child begin to gain a sense of progress in reading. If this automatization of items 4, 5 and 6 can be accomplished within a year of their introduction and acquisition, the child will be well on the way to some degree of skill in reading, far enough, at any rate, for it to be self-evident to the child that he is making progress.

The fact that the differentiation and identification of letter shapes and sounds are referred to in isolation from words, by no means implies that they should be taught in isolation. They are many ways of avoiding this, amongst others, Stott's use of Touch Cards and Morris Cards, Daniel's and Diack's missing letter, and the early games in Reis' *Fun with Phonics*. The inventive teacher can devise many ways of making this stage interesting and absorbing for the child.

The difficulties which arise here are not caused by the complexity of what the child sees, for there is ample evidence that children who have received suitable pre-reading training can deal with these visual complexities. There is reason to believe, however, that the difficulties are more likely to be caused by the necessity to associate, to order and to orientate the sounds relating to the visual symbols. Hence, the essential part that oral work should play in any reading programme. One example can be drawn from *Fun with Phonics* (Reis, 1962). Children have letters of the alphabet hung round their necks and on instructions from the teacher the particular letters of a given word move together, each making its relevant sound, until when close together a synthesis is achieved. Stott's Half Moon Cards perform much the same task, but it is important to vocalize the action as it is performed.

Item 6 introduces the idea of sequence and raises the question of whether this is a task too difficult for children in the very early stages of reading. Of course, much depends on the children and much may depend on the methods used. At any rate the reports of various workers in the field suggest that many children can, at surprisingly early ages, accomplish this task in that they have learnt to read (Downing, 1963); Lynn, 1963; Southgate, 1963; Doman, 1965). The research of Bruce (1964) does illustrate, however, some of the difficulties which may arise when children are introduced to reading instruction at an early age. Incidentally, Anderson (1954) disputes the contention that children below the age of 5 or 6 years lack the physical and physiological development of the eye necessary for reading. Whether or not it is worth bothering to achieve an early start, before the age of five or six years, is a different question altogether. Much will depend on the breadth and depth of the child's experiences, language as well as other types of experience, and upon the facility with which he learns to read. The child between the ages of three and five has so much to learn that it is very important not to overburden him by making additional demands upon him.

Once a child can identify three-letter sequences (items 4, 5 and 6), he has taken the first and crucial step in the acquisition of the phonic skills essential to adequate reading.

Items 8, 10 and 11 should be approached in much the same way as items 4 and 5, avoiding drudgery or methods that are too academic.

Items 9 and 12 involve great complexity of skill. All adult skilled readers have at one time or another faced the problem presented by unfamiliar or new words and it is enlightening to recall the difficulties. The child will be facing similar or enhanced difficulties on numerous occasions. In attacking these words the child will have to decode letter strings and store the vocalized form in the immediate memory store. This task will be more difficult if the string does not correspond to a known word, for the chances are high that the child will lose trace of what he is trying to retain, while concentrating upon the ensuing strings. For example, the three syllables of *yesterday* are probably easier to retain whilst searching for the whole word than the three syllables of *envelope*, simply because *yes* and *day* are known words in their own right, whereas not one of the syllables, *en*, *vel*, *ope*, have any individual meaning for the child. In order to help the child it is important (a) to encourage a confident approach, (b) to help the child to develop a searching attitude towards words and their constructions, and (c) to use programmes which aid the child. One programme of this type is that used in the *Royal Road Series*. Words featuring new phonic rules are introduced gradually and within a context

20

which helps to indicate to the child what his responses should be. Carver and Stowasser, in the *Oxford Colour Readers* use contextual aids, such as picture stories and illustrated situations, frequently of a humorous or ridiculous character, to help the child overcome the difficulties of synthesizing the sounds of the parts of some of the new words. Other schemes, like Stott's *Programmed Reading Kit*, Reis' *Fun with Phonics*, and Southgate and Havenhand's *Sounds and Words*, use games and exercises as an independent activity to introduce new and complex words.

Naturally, it would be undesirable to prescribe dogmatically a rigid scheme of work for dealing with the introduction of the sub-skills. So much will depend upon the children, the materials available, the organization and timetable of the school and, above all else, on the teacher. It would be impossible to include in one scheme or set of suggestions a programme suited to teachers of all types. The purpose of this chapter has been, therefore, to attempt to define the things that have to be accomplished by a child learning to read and, apart from some suggestions, leaving it to the teacher to work out methods which suit all the various factors operating in her particular case.

However, before leaving these sub-skills it is important to recall that they are *sub*-skills and do not add up to the total reading process. Reading is not merely skilled behaviour in the substitution of visuo-spatial cues by audio-temporal cues; it is interpretation of symbols true enough, but within a wider context of language. Meaning and structural form enter at every level—and hence the great importance of reading with a meaningful context. This implies that all aspects of the reading programme must be couched in language that is meaningful to the child. Whether one is teaching letters and their sounds, words or phrases, it is imperative that these should be presented at all times in language patterns which the child can easily understand. The writer's own research has indicated how strongly the reader relies upon anticipation of what lies ahead in the text. For example, after reading a word incorrectly, anticipation of the text to follow can be so strongly centred upon the misreading of that one word that the reader attempts to modify the text, even though it is well within his powers of interpretation. Therefore, unless the teacher is careful and ensures that the work she is presenting to the child is clearly understood in terms of the child's own language, there is danger of a chain of misinterpretations and the result will be utter confusion.

4

The organization of reading in the classroom

Having outlined in the last two chapters an explanation of skilled reading and the factors involved in learning to read, it is now possible to consider the more general conclusions and implications for classroom practice.

The beginning

Mention was made in the previous chapter of the need for the child to understand the nature of the task of reading. This cannot be taught in a very short space of time. It is acquired by the child through a variety of experiences; through seeing print in the classroom in the form of labels, notices, and descriptive tags, through stories read to the children by adults, through poems and rhymes in large print which are displayed and read by the teacher. Constant oral reference to print will gradually give the child some idea that print can be interpreted. This is a vital stage of preparation and it should not be rushed. All too frequently one finds teachers in our infant schools who have not really thought out its implications. It is not just a matter of letting children wallow in a rich environment; they must use that environment to bring children closer and closer to the interpretation of print.

23

One attempt to use the initial preparatory period in a constructive way is explained by Tansley (1967). He sees the need for training in perception and he suggests games and exercises in which the child has to place, eventually, various groups of objects in a required order proceeding from left to right. The idea behind this type of activity is, that in endeavouring to follow and comply with a sequence, the child will become so accustomed to the importance of order and a left to right orientation, that he will be well prepared to accept the importance of order and sequence when applied to words, sounds and letters. In fact, he does not stop at objects, but continues with the exercises in a different form, using words, later sounds, and finally letters as the manipulative objects of the exercises.

How far the use of objects, as distinct from words, sounds and letters is directly helpful as a preparation for reading is not clear. Undoubtedly, it is of some help in that groups of objects can be used, such as a family, with whose order the child is familiar. The exercise is then meaningful in itself and is not dependent upon an interpretation of third order symbolism. The degree of relevance to learning to read could well depend upon the amount of vocalization of thoughts and actions during the exercise. Discussing the order with another child, or better still with a teacher, could lead to increased insight into the significance of order and sequence.

When Tansley comes to the use of words, sounds and letters, there can be no doubt whatsoever about the importance of this type of training, because here he is dealing with the very substance of written language. In the early stages of the preparatory period, it will be for the teacher to take the initiative in the exercises: the

24

teacher will note aloud, in an incidental but informative manner, the order and sequence of words or phrases in a sentence which she has written or prepared in some way for the children; also, she will emphasize the initial sounds of words. Gradually, the children will take an increasingly dominant part in the exercises. They will repeat the words in the correct order, pick out the initial letters and the initial sounds, and generally begin to answer the teacher's questions rather than merely listen to her participating in the exercises. If this is done on an individual or small group basis, there will be no danger of the teacher 'leaping too far ahead' of the children. Slowly the whole emphasis will change and the child will now *do* the exercises. He will point to words on separate cards and place them in a desired order; he will copy words, using wooden letters, and he will do many more exercises similar to Tansley's. The over-riding consideration will be that these exercises should not become burdensome and, if possible, they should form an integral part of the more general work of the class.

Another effective way of using the preparatory period is by introducing writing, in the sense that the child begins to try to formulate single letters, either individually or in simple words. This, in itself, will make a considerable contribution to learning to read because, by learning to write individual letters, the child learns that each letter is invariable in shape and orientation. This alone is an achievement of learning, because up till this moment the child will have learned that orientation does not matter when concerned with objects. For example, it does not matter whether a cup is placed with its handle to the left or to the right, or indeed, whether the cup is upside down or on its side, it is still a cup. However, when the child comes to letters and words, orientation is vitally important; for example, a circle with the stalk on the left hand side instead of on the right is not an *a*; and a *c* on its back could look like a *u*

In addition, many people, Tansley and Fernald amongst them, have for long insisted that we should pay more attention to learning through the kinaesthetic sense. The very motion and movement of writing is a powerful means whereby we learn. Too often teaching techniques rely exclusively upon sight and hearing and neglect touch and movement. Any infant school which does not attach considerable importance to finger tracing for example, is depriving its children of a powerful aid to learning. Therefore, the formation of letters by both finger and by pencil should be encouraged from the earliest days in the infants school.

Teacher-child activities

However, it is obvious that the preparatory stage is not merely the use of one or two devices to aid learning. It is a period of time lasting maybe weeks or maybe months, in which it should be possible to introduce gradually an increasing amount of relevant pre-reading work.

As time passes, more specific attention can be given to labelling. This should not be a once-and-for-all action: 'There, we have put the word *door* on the door; whenever you want that word always look at the door'. In this way the word merely becomes part of the unnoticed environment, therefore, it is necessary to be constantly labelling and relabelling objects, talking about the appropriate labels, selecting them and noting their peculiarities. The teacher will take a predominant part in this activity at first, but as time goes on the child will take more and more of the initiative in selecting labels from the bundle. No label should remain on its object for more than a week. It should be taken down, talked about again and, if necessary replaced later—possibly the next day—by another child. By doing this, the child becomes involved in an action, and he must engage, either with the teacher or later alone, in the activities of perception, discrimination, association and selection in order to perform that act.

Whenever any activity such as this arises it is up to the teacher to be ready to deal with as many aspects of language and reading development as possible. What does the word mean? How can it be used? Are there several uses? What is its sound? What sound does it begin with? Does it remind you of anything? Do you notice any shapes in the word that you have seen before? All these questions can lead on to interesting discussions; but there are few teachers who possess the skill and spontaneity to be able to make the most of these situations unless they have prepared for them by thinking out the implications of each activity in terms of possible language development.

Many opportunities arise in the informal infants' classroom for using spoken language and introducing isolated words and phrases in several situations. No opportunity should be missed in calling a child's attention to words and their use. For example, an interesting and involved discussion recently took place in a reception class about the word *blow*. This word had appeared in a story and it referred to one person hitting another. One of the children, who obviously thought of this word in terms of air escaping from pursed lips expressed her bewilderment. The teacher took her point and an interesting study of the word *blow* developed. If opportunities such as this are allowed to pass, then not only is the opportunity for learning a word missed, but confusion is allowed to blur the child's concept of the word.

Indeed, one of the strongest arguments that can be put forward in support of the primary classroom where several different activities are taking place concurrently is that it provides the opportunity for the teacher to enter into intimate teaching situations with a small group of children. Here discussion can take place and, through oral communication, the teacher and child together will be able to probe more deeply any given problem.

Class organization

Much of the preparatory work is best done informally, because in this way it becomes a living part of the work of the children. Noting things about identical words, comparing similarities and differences between words which are similar in some ways but not identical, noting and making the sounds of words, identifying the initial sounds of words, all of these can be developed with a gradually increasing intensity within the framework of the normal activities in an informal classroom. They will arise out of discussions, activities, stories, and in many other ways. However the teacher has to be always on the look out for such opportunities, and unless she knows what she is looking for she will not know what to do when the occasion arises. In addition, this type of work can only be done effectively if the teacher has given considerable attention to the organization of the work of the class and to the arrangement of the physical features of the classroom. Intimacy can be achieved at story time with numbers up to forty and above, but with all the skill in the world it is virtually impossible to contrive the necessary atmosphere of purposeful participation, so necessary for the types of teaching situations which are now being considered, in groups of more than eight children. In fact some situations require individual attention whilst others demand groups of two, three or four children.

This means, of course, that there should be nothing static about the grouping of a class. Numbers should be continually changed to meet the requirements of each particular situation. Flexibility is all important and it can become the most effective attribute of the teacher, provided that the teacher is prepared to engage in a process of forward planning.

This is the difference between a planned and prepared educational situation and the haphazard chaos that sometimes passes for progressive education. The effective teacher is never afraid, provided the circumstances are appropriate, to pick up a point and teach to that point, whether it be to the class, to a group or to an individual child. But she always does it within an interesting, exciting and appropriate context.

Pre-reading in U.S.A. and Britain

In the United States of America during recent years considerable attention has been given to the use of pre-reading schemes of instruction. When one examines some of the exercises that the child is expected to do, one wonders at the relevance of many of them. Nevertheless, this does not mean that we should not give a great deal more thought to the preparatory stage of reading instruction. Perhaps we should see it not so much in the context of the acquisition of techniques, in the manipulation of

29

objects, shapes, lines and drawings, that can later be applied to learning to read a text, as in the context of language usage and its association with print. For example, reading is a matter not so much of knowing what a sequence is, but rather of seeing the significance of that sequence, when applied to letters and words, in terms of spoken language. Therefore, spoken language should be our starting point and from this there should develop gradually an association with a text in the form of words, sentences, letters, as may be appropriate at each particular stage.

Two codes of language

If, then, language is to be the basis of our work, we cannot ignore the fact that Bernstein (1960) found two codes of language usage. The elaborated code, which is the form of language used in formal situations by teachers and lecturers in order to convey an intellectual or otherwise formal message, finds greater use amongst the middle classes. It can be loosely described as grammatically correct language with no omissions, such as can be found in text books and in journalism of the type that is found in the *Guardian*, *The Times*, and the *New Statesman*. The restricted code, which is the language of intimate informal communication, is the language which passes amongst close intimates and members of a family. It relies heavily upon close interpersonal relationships and contains many omissions and shortened forms of language, which if inserted would greatly inhibit the warmth of communication. Whilst this restricted code is used to some extent by the educated middle classes, it is used more widely by members of the working classes.

30

All teachers are aware of the advantages which a middle class child from a cultured and educated home background has over the child from the culturally deprived uneducated home, whether it be working or middle class—and we should not forget that many prosperous houses are sadly deficient so far as educated conversation and interests are concerned. But do we make sufficient allowances for this in school? The research of Goodacre (1967) suggests that we do not; in her sample of urban schools she found that 'broadly speaking the social area of the school had little effect upon teaching methods, materials, standards, or even school conditions'. This is a most disturbing fact, for it means that teachers are not differentiating between the difficulties of a child who has some familiarity with the use of formal English, who can express himself in clear and precise terms, and the child whose English is little more than a series of phrases, blunt and lacking in the fine distinctions required to convey ideas and thoughts which have some continuity. It clearly emphasizes the message of Bereiter and Engelmann (1966), that if we do not do something that is radically compensatory for the child who is at a disadvantage, how can we ever hope for him to catch up with his more fortunate contemporaries.

It is obvious, therefore, that one of the prime concerns of the infant school should be to detect deficiencies in language and, by greater emphasis on the spoken word, help to rectify them. This means a greater emphasis on communication between teacher and child. Time must be found to help those who need it; but above all, plans must be worked out in which there is a clear emphasis upon getting the child to listen to, and to practise using, a more elaborated code in situations where the relationships between the participants are conducive to the development of this code. This may be for only a few minutes every day, but frequency and practice are essential if any substantial help is to be given to children from homes where they receive little that is helpful in learning to use the English language as they meet it in their reading books.

Look-and-say

The preparatory period does not consist solely of familiarization with language and its loose association with sounds, words and phrases. It has been wrongly thought in the past that when a child began to read his first book, that the preparatory period was over and that formal instruction in reading had begun. This attitude has tended to confuse our understanding of the whole process of learning to read. It is the object of this book, therefore, to draw a sharp distinction between the essential contribution of look-and-say as a preparatory and highly motivational introduction to reading, and its inadequacies as a method of teaching children to read.

Obviously, from what has been written in the two previous chapters, look-and-say, or the whole word method, plays little if any part as an aid to learning to read as such, because it does not help a child to decode unfamiliar words unaided. It does, however, provide an invaluable introductory stage in which the child is prepared for the task of learning to read: he learns to recognize a few familiar words, although he cannot make fine distinctions between words of similar graphemic pattern; he gains some knowledge of the sense of purpose in print; he learns to operate in a left to right sequence if two or more words are strung together; he begins to develop a notion of correspondence, albeit a hazy one, between sound and symbol; and he can achieve a form of 'reading' which, although it merely means that he can loosely recognize a few familiar words, does have deep motivational significance, in so much as a child who thinks he can accomplish a task is more likely to do so with greater ease than one who does not. If this distinction, between the preparatory function of look-and-say and learning to read itself, is maintained, it is possible to gain a clearer appreciation of the exact process of learning to read.

A brief account of some responses of young children under the age of five will illuminate the need to go further in our teaching of reading than the initial recognition of whole words, invaluable though that may be as an introduction to print.

A child of exactly four years noted the *snakey shapes*—*s*, and was intrigued to learn that it said *'ss*. The same child referred to the *curly letter with a stalk* when looking at the *a* at the beginning of *apple*. A three-year-old recognized her own and her mother's initial letters in the abbreviated form of saint—*ST*—but confused the letters with the whole names. Similarly there are cases of three-year-olds recognizing *monkey* by the *m* and the *y*, and later confusing the words *monkey* and *mummy*. The important point illustrated here is that children before they can read begin to make a detailed study of letter shapes and sounds within a word. And it is this very fact—that children are noticing letters—which causes a very dangerous situation to arise. It is obvious that children are going to use letter cues, even if we only show them whole words, as was the case of the three-year-old mentioned above. If they receive no help with these cues then, as was evident in the confusion of *monkey* and *mummy* and the interchange of initial letter and whole words for the names of mother and daughter, they are apt to use the cues wrongly in some instances. So, in using a look-and-say method, the unwary teacher may even encourage the learning of errors by inviting the pupil to read the word on the basis of his recognition of one or two letters and without regard for the other parts of the word.

LEARNING TO READ

The child having been prepared for learning to read must now learn to read. That is, the child must learn how to decode words which he does not recognize 'on sight', by attaching sounds to the parts and meaning to the whole. He must incorporate the sub-skills into easy usage.

The use of books

The sub-skills cannot be effectively and quickly learnt by using reading books alone. It would be impossible to incorporate within one reading book, or even two or three books, both a text that is interesting and that gives adequate instruction or help with the sub-skills. A planned programme in which these component skills are taught independently of the reading books is, therefore, necessary. The reading books, if planned in close conjunction with this programme, can then be used for practice, consolidation and enjoyment. This has the advantage of separating the frustrations and difficulties of learning a skill—and only a naïve teacher would deny that these frustrations and difficulties do occur in the case of every child from time to time—from the enjoyment of the fruits of that skill. It also means that books from their

34

earliest introduction can contain text which makes sense and involves a sequence of thought so that the processing of the perceptual input is made easier for the child. Very little sense can be made out of the text of many early primers in Britain and the United States of America. Robert Hall (1961) derisively mimics an introductory book: 'Spot! Jane! Look! Oh, Spot! Oh, Jane! Oh, look! Oh, Spot, Jane, look! Oh, oh, Spot, Spot, Jane, Jane, look, look! Oh, oh, oh, look, Spot, look, Jane, oh, Jane, oh, look, Spot, look, oh . . .!' In Britain, three of the most widely used primers—The Happy Venture Readers, The Janet and John Books, and The Ladybird Key Words Reading Scheme—have introductory books which consist of a series of sentences through which there runs no sequence or development in the story. The over-riding design lies in the introduction and repetition of words and phrases.

These books are in effect teaching devices; they are not meant to be reading books in the sense that a child can obtain information, unaided, from the text alone. The illustrations are intended to stimulate a line of thought, leading up to the learning of isolated words or phrases which accompany the picture. Whilst this procedure may arouse the interest of the child if conducted on an individual teaching basis, or even with very small groups of children, it does not present the teacher with the opportunities for an adequate programme of teaching. Therefore, these books fail to achieve two objectives; they make neither interesting reading for the child, nor are they a sufficient teaching device, especially when it is remembered that the apparatus which accompanies these early readers is almost invariably based on a look-and-say method, and consists merely of further pictures and words to be presented as wholes for matching.

The need for a programme

Children need to be prepared for reading in a more thorough fashion than this. They need a programme which has clearly defined objectives, carefully worked out so that every stage leads easily on to the next. A short book tagged on to the beginning of a set of readers is not by any means satisfactory. The child should not be expected to learn by means of magic, and it should not be assumed that because so many children learn with ease to read, that a programme of this kind is unnecessary. Such a programme should help the brighter children to learn even more easily, and it would provide those who do not find it so easy with a more substantial basis for learning. Much could be learnt from the principles of programmed learning where every step is a small one, none of these vital steps are missed out, and the gradient of learning is very gradual. Until a subject has been broken down into all its parts, it is very easy to by-pass essential parts or sub-skills which are necessary to the whole. Hence it is the thesis of this book that a substantial part of a programme of instruction and learning should be based upon the list of reading sub-skills.

This does not imply rigidity in the execution of the programme; it merely means that the teacher should have in her mind a general pattern upon which she can base the progress of each individual child. Each stage would be introduced only when the teacher thought that the child would be receptive to it. A dogmatic and inflexible adherence to a lifeless scheme of work should not be the objective. In order to achieve maximum effect, this programme should be planned by each individual teacher, in co-operation with other teachers who will teach the child during the period of his learning to read. Much of it could be done through games and interesting exercises. Above all the main objective should be the constant participation of the child. It is only by examining words, constructing words, examining their parts, building new words, using words, that the child can truly and effectively learn to read.

Two major problems

There are two major problems which face the child during the early stages of learning to read. One is the fact that, in English, more than one sound may be attached to some letters or letter strings, and vice versa. The initial teaching alphabet is a device which is intended to reduce the difficulty by making all but a few letters correspond to one sound only. Other devices that are being tried at the present time include the use of colour and the use of diacritical marks. Whether such innovations are justified can only be considered in conjunction with the wider aspects of learning, unlearning and the secondary effects on other skills such as spelling and writing. Therefore it is not intended to shorten and thereby weaken the discussion of this important problem here.

The point that emerges is that, either the teacher must accept and use one of these devices, or she must take specific and determined steps to teach the child that certain letters and digraphs will vary their sound according to the word in which they appear. Similarly, that some sounds will vary their letters. The possibility of confusion cannot be ignored, and only teaching of one kind or another will help the child to become familiar with the variant sounds of these letters. The teachers who prefer

37

to use the traditional spelling will find encouragement in some research by Levin (1963), from which he concludes that it is better to introduce irregularities of this type during the early stages because, although this may create initial difficulties, the child will be more adequately prepared mentally to meet new irregularities as they occur in the future.

These teachers will have two decisions to take:

1. Whether or not to teach the various sounds that can be attached to say, *ea*, in isolation from words; and

2. Whether more than one of these various sounds should be introduced simultaneously, for example, $/i:/$ and $/i:æ/$ in *beak* and *idea*.

The answer to the first point must surely be that only by including the sound in a word is it possible to emphasize its sound-function. Therefore, although the teacher may wish to give periods of drill in the *ea* $= /i:/$ sound—one period seldom seems enough—this could be more easily and meaningfully accomplished through the use of such words as *sea*, *beat*, *meat*, and so on. By this procedure the child will be given the necessary repetition in sounding *ea*; and she will be given, at the same time, some understanding of the part which this digraph plays in certain words. Reinforcement and learning will be the result of a combination of repetition and insight, and by using both sound and word right from the beginning of the exercise the two will have developed side by side, rather than repetition running ahead of insight and understanding. Indeed, throughout the period of learning to read it is important to remember that it is not merely a matter of knowing the right response to a symbol; the child must perceive ways in which he can use that response. For example, the sound $/i:/$, as in *sea* on its own, means

38

nothing and is functionless, but once it is placed with certain other letters, as in *sea, beat, meat*, it performs a function and it contributes to a meaningful unit.

The second decision concerns a problem which has caused much argument, but which has led to no research so far. Therefore, all we can do is try to rationalize the argument. When the sound of *ea* is /i:/, it appears only in certain words; in others where the letters *ea* appear, a different sound must be attached. There are two ways of dealing with this: one is to know that when *t* proceeds *ea* and *rs* follow it, then the sound of *ea* is /i:/; the other way is to know the various sounds of *ea* and, by means of experimentation and deduction, to arrive at the appropriate sound. The former way seems to be the only viable solution, because the latter entails maintaining in the mind, during these very early stages, two or more alternative sounds with which the child is not familiar; and to use them under these circumstances involves a degree of abstract thought on the part of the child, which lies beyond his abilities at this stage of development (assuming that the child is approximately five or six years old). Hence, it follows that it would be better to concentrate upon one sound for a letter or digraph at a time, proceeding to an alternative sound only when the first sound is known in the context of several words.

When the child comes to practise his skill in distinguishing the various sounds of a particular letter or digraph, it is imperative that the context should clearly and unquestionably help him, otherwise he will easily become confused—it is so easy to lose newly acquired knowledge at this stage—and an incorrect response means that a considerable amount of re-learning and reinforcement then becomes necessary. If *ea* is to be practised, then the words containing the letters *ea* should appear in sentences, the meaning of which limits the chance of an incorrect response. For example,

> Our class *team beat* class three.
> You may sit *near* your friend.
> May I have an apple *please?*

The other problem is much more complex in itself. It concerns the child's ability to see groups of letters within a word, to attach a particular combination of sounds to that group and, by doing this, to by-pass the laborious (and in some case impossible) task of blending the separate letters into the required complex sound. For example, in the word *train*, /t/ and /r/ do not make /tr/, at least not as any child would recognize it. Therefore, until the child perceives *tr* as a single unit, that child is labouring under extreme difficulty.

This all connects closely with Gibson's work, mentioned earlier, in which she showed how important it is to see the letter group as a unit in terms of sound. But there are other pieces of research which add weight to our concern for this particular problem. Chall *et al.* (1963) found that ability in auditory blending at the age of six years (entry to school in the United States of America) significantly affected silent reading ability in the third year of school. However, she did not know whether this ability could be trained by direct instruction; neither did she know whether lack of blending ability was the result of inability to blend sounds together or of poor or inaccurate perception. All she could say was that blending ability and reading ability were closely related.

The work of Blank and Bridger (1966) suggests that the ability to match audial and visual patterns is not so much the difficulty of integration, as suggested by Birch and Belmont (1963) and Birch and Lefford (1964), but of attaching a sound label to the visual information received —that is, of knowing the letter or letter string well enough to attach some kind of name or label to it.

Associated with this problem is the necessity for the child to hold in mind the wholeness of a word, phrase or sentence, whilst attending to the individual parts (Goins, 1958).

These separate pieces of research and the general experiences of teachers do not give us the complete answer to our problem. They do, however, indicate some of the considerations we should bear in mind when dealing with children at this stage. We should not allow much time, if any, to elapse between learning to identify letter shapes by their sound (sub-skills numbers 4 and 5) and learning to identify letter clusters by their sound (sub-skills numbers 7, 8, 10 and 11). In fact the two should proceed more or less simultaneously, and it would be beneficial to break away from the idea that only after the child has spent a considerable time on single letter unit words (in the sense that *cat* consists of three single letter units, *c*, *a*, *t*), can he then be introduced to multiple letter units (as in *train*, where *tr*, *ai* and *n* form the units). No reading that the child will do can possibly be confined to words consisting solely of single letter units; and as it is virtually impossible to build up such words as *train* and *field* from the separate letter sounds, then some form of help in grouping must be given to aid the child in the early stages. And it is in the early stages that the child needs help as frequently and as continuously as possible. It is interesting to note that the initial teaching alphabet goes some way to incorporating this principle into the written symbolization

41

of the language, with such units as ch, sh, η, but it still leaves a lot of grouping to the child and the teacher. Hence, whatever the medium, traditional or i.t.a. an effort must be made to help the child to cope with this difficult problem.

Learning words

Another important consideration, which leads on from all this, is the manner of presentation of words. It is clear from the work of Gibson and Goins that considerable importance should be attached to presenting letters and letter clusters within the context of complete words. However, every teacher knows that this is difficult to do in practice.

In an earlier chapter, reading was referred to as a linguistic skill, which means that it is closely connected with language. Now it is assumed by some that, just as a language is learnt by a method of contrastive discrimination (a term used by Ronald Morris)—that is, by incidentally comparing and contrasting words as we sound them —so children should be taught to read by causing them to discriminate between words and never to separate the sounds within those words. Some linguists favour this approach and it is, of course, theoretically and linguistically sound. But the situation in which a child learns to talk is far different from that in which he learns to read. When learning to talk he is, from the moment he wakes until he falls asleep again at night, using words, phrases and sentences. He is continuously talking to his mother, his friends and to himself, and his mother and his friends are responding and reacting to his efforts. He experiments with sounds and words, imitates those who have skill in

42

spoken language, and adapts that which he finds useful for his own purposes. All the time he is, unconsciously in a sense, making contrasts and discriminations, deciding what is feasible and what is not in each particular language situation, erasing mistakes and reinforcing correct responses. The success of learning by contrastive discrimination depends upon this constant practice and participation.

This is not possible when learning to read in school. There are too many other things vying for an equal, if not superior, place in his attention. Learning to talk becomes part of every activity of the child, and there seems to be an inner drive which spurs him on to practise more and more. This is not so with learning to read. By its very nature it cannot be part of everything a child does in school. Neither can the teacher play a similar role to that of the mother: she has not the time for constant interaction with one child. Therefore a compromise is necessary, because it would be absolutely impossible for a teacher to provide such frequent and relevant practice to enable the child to build up a sufficient density of learning situations in order to make the contrasts. In these circumstances, whilst not reverting to the old method of adding letter sound to letter sound, for example $/k/ + /l/ + /i/ + /n/ + /g/ = /kliŋ/$ (*cling*), nevertheless it is necessary to allow some summation. When this is done, care should be taken not to over-emphasize the isolation of each phoneme—the gaps between them should not be accentuated to any degree—and, wherever possible, a contrast with another word or words should be drawn. By doing this it will be possible to retain contrastive discrimination as the basic method of learning new words, and yet to provide the child with a superimposed device for tackling words when he is uncertain of their pronunciation.

Yet when the teacher has decided how to present words to the child, there remains the problem of which words to use. Naturally, these words should be closely associated with the child's interests in general. But should they be dissimilar in structure as the look-and-say enthusiasts believed?—they maintained that in presenting words such as *elephant* and *cat* side by side, the child would more easily discriminate between the two words because of the added cue of difference in length—or should these words be similar in structure and, thereby, force the child to look more closely at the letters of the word, as Daniels and Diack maintain?

Samuels and Jeffrey in 1966 and 1967 report two experiments which examine the problem of learning words and then transferring this knowledge to the identification of new words. They suggest that if we select words which are highly similar, such as *cat* and *cap*, the child will become accustomed to making careful discriminations, which he can only do by looking at all the letters in the word. If, however, we select dissimilar words, then the child is morely likely to try to read new words by looking at less than all the letters in the word.

It seems imperative, therefore, that the teacher should frequently introduce groups of words with a similar structure, if for no other reason than to inculcate a habit of close scrutiny of the parts of the words. Every child has to learn that reading, in the early stages, cannot be approached in a haphazard way: it is only by serious attention to detail that the child is able to keep to the gist of the text.

Order and orientation

During the early stages of learning to read, the child has to acquaint himself with the part which order and a left to right orientation play. Vernon (1957) suggested that this could be the source of some difficulty. Obviously a child must learn the significance of moving from left to right, for until he does he will find the whole business of reading confusing and virtually impossible. The child's understanding of a left to right orientation and the importance of order in written English is not, however, a thing that can be intellectualized by the young child. A teacher cannot say, 'We go from left to right and each letter and sound has to be in its correct place', and expect the child to understand to the extent of being able to recall and use this knowledge on a future occasion. It is something that the child comes to understand gradually, by constantly hearing sounds and words, by watching the teacher and parent read aloud (so much the better if at this stage the adult periodically follows the print with the forefinger) and by copying words and short phrases or sentences written and read aloud by the teacher. There may come a stage when the teacher may express this in intellectual terms, as in the above statement, but it will only be understood at a particular and advanced stage in the child's progress towards understanding and then only in terms of his own experience through active participation in conjunction with an adult reader. This applies in the case of all the sub-skills of reading.

However, an over-emphasis on a left to right sequence can inhibit, slow down, and even prevent the child from obtaining meaning from a text. The child will learn to read more effectively depending upon the degree to which he integrates and uses the three aspects of language—the perceptuo-motor or phonic aspect, the syntactic and the semantic aspects. Therefore, the words must be meaningful and familiar, the style must be simple and closely akin to the child's, and the text must develop in an easily discernible sequence. And this, as has already been stated, should be so from the earliest book. Furthermore, the child should be shown how to use the various known clues in the text in order to interpret the unknown ones. For example, in the sentence *Dora nursed the doll*, let us assume that the child knows all the words except *nursed*. It should be part of the teacher's task to demonstrate ways of deducing the possible meanings of the verb in this sentence by pondering the connection between the subject and object, and adding to this some clues from the letters of the word, such as the first letter-sound, or better still, the first three letter-sounds, and, in the case of polysyllabic words, picking out any syllable that is recognized. This, of course, implies breaking the strict left to right sequence. The child must 'hop about' seeking cues wherever they are to be found, whilst retaining the need to process the facts gained into a left to right sequence.

Again we see the need for active participation by the child: working with words and manipulating them as in some of the exercises recommended by Fries, Wilson and Rudolph (1966), Daniels and Diack (1960) and Stott (1962). Perhaps it would be true to say that the main contribution to learning to read made by Gattegno is not his use of colour but the way in which children are taught to manipulate the signals obtained from the letters of words. Every student should see the film of Dr Gattegno teaching a group of children to read, but they should be expected afterwards to consider it within the context of an informal infant classroom.

The cyclic process

It is always helpful for a teacher to have some framework of teaching technique, within which it is possible to couch the full programme of instruction and learning. Whitehead (1962) suggested a cyclic process of learning: stage one, he called romance, stage two, precision and stage three generalization. If the teacher uses these as a general guide to each phase of the work and bases the teaching programme upon them, there need be no drudgery or sterile work. Each phase, whether it is short like the introduction of a letter or a digraph, or a much longer task like the acquisition of the ability to synthesize meaningless vocal syllables (item 9 in the list of sub-skills), should be introduced in the most enthusiastic and intriguing manner possible. At this stage of romance the child's attitude to the learning task is established, and it is important that he should look forward to this task with as much excitement as possible. It will help if it is remembered that children love to acquire exclusive knowledge; they enjoy learning about anything that fits into a pattern or is peculiar in any way, and they can easily catch the enthusiasm of a teacher. No work should be introduced without a serious attempt to catch the interest and curiosity of the children. Naturally this stage can be overdone, just as it can be neglected, but it is after all part of the teacher's skill to be continually readjusting her teaching in the light of her experience.

The stage of precision is where the child actually learns something. In learning to read, it is the stage where the

47

child learns the sub-skills of reading and to interpret the phonic, syntactic and semantic aspects of written language. The teaching must show the children how they can remember words by acquiring a regular procedure which they can automatically adopt with each new word. Fernald (1943) invented a particularly thorough form for doing this: by tracing, vocalizing and writing each new word. But there are simpler ways, the most popular being to look, vocalize the syllables, and say each word. The form which a teacher uses will depend on the children and the teacher's requirements.

Numerous opportunities will arise at this stage for integrating work on sub-skills into a wider context of individualized developmental learning within a rich and engrossing environment.

The teacher may be discussing sounds—sea sounds, country sounds, town sounds, musical sounds, and she may notice that one of the class or group is beginning to revel in the vocal sensation produced by the /ʃ/ sound in words such as *splash*, *lash*, *crash*. The opportunity is made for discussing the blending of two letters into one new sound. Much will then depend upon the individual child and his intellectual relationship with the group. If the group forms a loosely homogeneous unit, then they can all benefit, some more than others, from dealing specifically with this blending process. If all the group are not more or less at the same level, then further re-grouping will be necessary. As to the way in which the teaching should be done, each teacher will develop individual techniques, and naturally some will be more effective than others, but provided that boredom is avoided, any attempt to help the child will be better than leaving it to chance. Perhaps the only basic guide for teachers is that the sounds should be taught as they stand within words and sentences, rather than as isolated phonemes devoid of contextual meaning.

This type of procedure, where the teacher picks from an interesting discussion or activity a problem which faces the child and then attempts to give the child greater insight into the system of written language, is an excellent example of the opportunities for relating skills which have to be learnt to the wider aspects of language usage. Not only will the children have enjoyed the discussion of sounds and all the imagery that may be called up; they will have seen the relevance of symbols in helping to express and formulate some of these ideas in a written form.

Nothing should be allowed to spoil a good story or discussion, but if there can be a follow up or an innocuous diversion by means of which the child's skill is extended, then so much more will have been achieved. The child will enjoy his new skill, for it will have been presented to him in a meaningful and relevant context.

It cannot be emphasized too strongly or too frequently that it would be dangerous for a teacher to take the sub-skills and proceed to exercise the child in each in quick succession in the hope of achieving a rapid rate of progress in learning to read. Such a course would be disastrous and totally out of keeping with all that is known and felt about primary education. A child can only understand the intricacies of written language if his interest in the whole process is aroused, if he is given adequate instruction and guidance in assimilating this knowledge, and if he is given time to do so. Time may be a more important factor than we realize. Indeed it may well be that in the past we have placed emphasis rightly upon the motivational and the instructional aspects of learning to read but that we have inadvertently ignored those aspects of our teaching programmes which should allow for the effective assimilation of facts and skills that are discovered and learned. For no matter how well a child learns, say, the sound of a particular letter, that knowledge is of little use until the child has learnt to understand and appreciate the function of that letter sound in relation to other letter sounds. If experimentation means anything it means the handling of known facts to achieve further knowledge, and the better we are able to arrange this experimentation by the child the more effective will be the resultant learning. Therefore, it is absolutely essential for the teacher to plan the work of her class in such a way that within the wider programme of educating her class—with all that this implies in a progressive school—she is able to ensure that each child is unobtrusively taught the sub-skills of reading. The more effective and skilful the teacher, the more difficult it will be for an outside observer to discern the usual trimmings of any set or rigid programme. Flexibility will be the key note. Having a programme as a model in mind, the effective teacher will then be ready to take every opportunity as it arises to teach the child to read, to acquire the skills of identification and comprehension. It is a process that cannot be rushed, but one which can be presented with varying degrees of effectiveness.

And whilst the particular aspects of word recognition are being learnt, there must occur a deepening acquaintance with, and knowledge of, the structure of language and the meanings which can be derived from that structure. This is part of the process of learning to read which frequently tends to neglected. Children are taught to recognize words and then are sometimes left to acquire incidentally an ability to interpret the sum total of these words. It is depressing to reflect upon the degree of skill with which language is taught in most primary schools, yet if a child is to become a skilled reader, he must be able to extract fine distinctions in meaning from the written text, and this can only be done by the child if he has a rich background of oral language. The findings of Bernstein should not be ignored; no school should maintain the pretence that all children at a particular age are equally equipped with the language facility necessary for learning to read with ease.

The stage of generalization is roughly the point at which the child uses what he has learnt. It may take the form of practice or the accomplishment of some feat. It may involve repeating or reading a single word or it may involve reading a sentence, a passage, or a whole book. It does not necessarily come at the end of a lesson: it can occur several times during a lesson. In any case it should involve enjoyment through performance based on the acquisition of a new skill.

Clearly, Whitehead's pattern is compatible with the separation of a programme of instruction from the reading of books. Much of the latter will come into the stage of generalization and this is surely its rightful place. Unless the child sees reading as an enjoyable pursuit, he will not, after the first surge of enthusiasm has passed, be sufficiently interested in the task itself to continue without some form of external motivation. And where external motivation has to be employed, the endeavours to produce another willing and enthusiastic reader will be at the point of failure.

The question of what is feasible within the time available raises the question of the apportionment of that time.

One important consideration is that the effectiveness of the teaching is not a function of the length of time spent in any one period on learning to read, but rather it is a function of the frequency of the instruction, up to a certain limit. Thus, two ten-minute periods of instruction and learning per day are better than one period of twenty minutes, and in many instances four five-minute periods are better still. Anyone who has watched children during reading lessons will know how little of the time is spent in concentrating upon the subject matter to be learnt. Children just cannot concentrate for long periods of time (Huey, in a very useful book on primary education, mentions that maintaining near-point focus for long periods causes strain and leads to distraction), and with the disappearance of rigid time-tables and the introduction of a variety of simultaneous activities, there is no longer any need for the teacher to waste her energy trying to make the child do something that is an impossibility. Short, lively bursts are far more effective; more is learnt in them, and their greater frequency reduces the time in which the material can be forgotten.

Games

Finally, a brief word about the use of games to enliven the learning process. These are frequently used with outstanding success (Reis, 1962 and Stott, 1964), but a word of caution is necessary. Many teachers will know how flat and uninteresting games can sometimes become. This is usually because the games for those particular children no longer give a sense of involvement and fulfilment, and it is these two factors which hold the interest and concentration of the children, not the fact that they may collect more cards than their opponent. Only adults have the maturity to withstand such boring pursuits, in the expectation of later rewards; children require to be so engaged in the task that they are positively achieving something at every step. Therefore, it is necessary for the teacher to be discriminating in the provision of games. They should suit the stage and temperament of the child and they should not be used indiscriminately or continuously. Much can be achieved by withdrawing games from use after a short period of time and then re-introducing them later. Children always find the contents of a cupboard more interesting than the materials on the open table.

Language patterns

Several people have argued the cases for and against the use of a controlled vocabulary in children's primers. It would be difficult to justify the indiscriminate use of an uncontrolled vocabulary; therefore, it would be more profitable to try to select books in which the authors have used vocabulary control, without sacrificing the style and interest of the story, and in a way which allows the child to compare and contrast words of a similar construction. For example, the simple story, 'Jane made a cake and gave it to Joe', draws the child's attention to the effects of the final *e* in these words.

A point about the use of books, which needs serious consideration in some future research, is the implications of using more than one set of readers or of adding supplementary readers, written by another author, to the main set that is in use. It has been noticed that some children, when reading at approximately Book Three level (about R.A. 7yrs.), do not read the equivalent books by other authors with the same ease and fluency. When this was first noticed it was thought to be the result of unfamiliar words. However, there is now some reason to believe that it may be the result of the use of a slightly different language structure in the books outside the basic scheme. Several years ago, when teaching juniors who were backward in reading and who had spent an undue amount of time on the Happy Venture Books, I noticed a tendency of some of the children to write their stories in the style of these books. These two instances point to the possibility that children are more susceptible to style and language structure than we imagine, and, at the early stages, where they are becoming accustomed to a particular style, the sudden introduction of a new style may cause some confusion.

This raises the question of when it is advisable to introduce the child to a different style. Obviously, if the child is to become an effective reader, he must become accustomed to various styles and to variations in language structure. But it is equally important not to introduce unnecessary impediments to progress at this early and critical stage.

The safest way of dealing with this problem is for each teacher to examine carefully the style and language structure of the reading books that she is using and, where changes occur, to prepare the children by introducing them to these variations independently of the books.

5

Reading in the junior school

It is being increasingly realized that it is not enough merely to take children to the stage where they can read simple straightforward prose, hoping that their skill will develop almost unaided. In the past the only aids used to increase the children's reading ability were in the form of some dictionary work, comprehension exercises and reading connected with work on projects. In many cases, these concessions made only a minor contribution to increased reading skill.

The dictionary work varied from indescribably bad to a fairly exacting study of word meanings. The reading connected with project work was frequently too loose and uncontrolled and therefore lacked rigour, making very little demand upon discriminative reading. The comprehension exercises frequently seemed purposeless and sterile. Children must have wondered at the sanity of adults who required them to read a text, which was not only about a donkey, but which mentioned the word on almost every line, and then when they answered the first question, 'What is this story about?' with the simple statement, 'A donkey', thought such penetrating insight on the part of the child worthy of a tick. Very few books of comprehension exercises are worth buying: their only value seems to be as a means of keeping the class quiet while the teacher does something else. Surely, there are other ways of doing this which would also be profitable to the children!

FUTURE PRACTICE

This state of affairs will almost certainly change in the next few years and, provided much thought is given to the change, it could have a profound effect upon the whole education of our children. More and more, we are coming to realize that a rich environment is not enough for primary school children: they need to develop certain facilities and skills in order that they may derive all the benefits from such an environment. Unfortunately these cannot be left to develop spontaneously. They have to be fostered through guidance and practice. The child has to be shown how to use his environment—his history books, his mathematical apparatus, his projects and centres of interest—and he has to develop particular skills in order to make the optimum use of all the interesting things that are before him.

In this chapter it is proposed to examine how the child's reading ability can be developed within the common programme of junior schools, so that the atmosphere of excitement to be found in an enriched environment is sharpened by a more sophisticated use of the opportunities which are provided. Later, in Chapter Six, another aspect of this problem of increased reading ability will be considered.

Word study

Word-recognition sounds such a dull pursuit, and perhaps that is why it has had very little place in the junior school. This need not be so, especially if care is taken in the presentation of the lessons and time is not wasted in tedious exercises.

When discussing look-and-say methods in an earlier chapter, it was stated that a place could be found for it as a means of increasing the speed of recognition of familiar words and of building up confidence in the ability to recognize these words by reduced cues; that is, by something less than a complete oral analysis of the word. Flash cards and the tachistoscopic presentation of words, phrases and sentences could be used well into the junior school, especially in the first and second years. Care should be taken not to spend more than five, or at most ten, minutes per session on this type of activity, but if it is carried out frequently, it will influence the children's attitude to the recognition of words. They will lose their fear of words and get out of the habit of unnecessarily slow recognition. Nila Banton Smith's story of Puccini and the organ-grinder (1966) admirably illustrates how useful it is to be jolted out of habits which are becoming established.

It should not be forgotten, however, that word recognition does not depend solely upon acquaintance with word forms. It depends also upon an understanding of them. This calls for a programme of word study. It need not be a formally prepared programme; in fact many teachers would wish to feel free to deal with words which arose out of a wider context of class activities. Nevertheless, the study of words must be a part of the work in

English. Children often show great interest in word building and word derivation if these are presented in a lively manner for short spells and at moments of optimum interest in the use of the word. The aim of this course of study should be to give the child an increasing insight into the construction of words; a knowledge of how they have developed will add greatly to the interest in their construction. Gradually this study of words will develop into a study of the place of words in a text; how various categories of words can be used and how they cannot be used; how the structure of the sentence can affect the meaning of the word. This will eventually link up with the proposed study of written language through comprehension exercises of one form or another.

Comprehension through reading books

In the earlier chapters the case was made for early reading books with more closely knit text which developed as a sequence of thought, rather than a series of loosely related episodes. This idea can now be expanded to cover reading in the junior schools. Whilst there is a great deal to be said for allowing children a wide choice in their reading—for how can we know what interests all the children have at a particular moment—there is also a great need to introduce gradually more discipline into reading as children grow older. How can they ever progress beyond Enid Blyton unless they are guided in their demands upon books?

One way in which this can be done is by making available reading books whose writers have some claim to the title of author. Many of these books exist and some are reasonably priced. Particularly high standards are set in the Puffin and Young Puffin books.

However, merely to place these books in the classroom does not seem to be enough. The child's awareness of the subtleties of the contents, the creation of atmosphere, the arousal of feelings, and of how situations are delineated and clarified by the careful and particular use of language, all have to be fostered by the help of an adult. At every stage in the junior school, this process can be started by asking a small group of children to read a book or short story and then to discuss it in the presence of the teacher, so that such things as reaction to the story, sympathy for and association with the characters, effectiveness of scenes or actions and how they were described, use of noticeable words and phrases, can all be examined in closer detail. Later, in the upper junior classes, short stories, chapters and passages from a book can be treated in a similar manner, but with increasing attention to details of style.

For those teachers who think this would be taking academic study too far, it should be remembered that even infants vary in their reactions to stories and in their love of words.

This kind of study will increase the child's ability to appreciate what he reads, especially if it is remembered that the reader's reaction to a text is a very personal one.

The personality of each child enters into these reactions and, therefore, any work of this nature must retain an intimacy in which the individual's reactions are respected. No child should be told his reactions are wrong; it is far better to let him hear of the reactions of the other children and the teacher, so that he can reassess, rather than reject, his own thoughts and feelings. In order to achieve the appropriate intimacy which this type of study demands, it seems inevitable that small groups of no more than six children should be used.

Comprehension as part of discovery

This is one side of reading for understanding. There is another: the extraction of exact meaning from carefully prepared passages. One might think that this is the old type of comprehension exercises with a fanciful name. But something far more exacting and purposeful is envisaged. Pieces of prose or poetry, prepared for use as comprehension passages, and their accompanying questions, should be constructed in a way that makes the children use the text to think out the answers. The answers should only be obvious to those who have followed the ideas of the text with care and understanding, and they should represent a form of discovery.

As the child progresses through the junior school the exercises should become more demanding and engrossing. Increasingly fine discriminations in meaning would have to be made, and at the end of the exercise the child should have learnt something of interest or value. The whole operation should not end as a mere exercise, but should lead up to the achievement of knowledge in one form or another. Many schools are already finding the S.R.A. reading laboratories exceedingly useful for this purpose. They contain some excellent material and they make some exacting demands upon the reader. However, there is a great need for more of this type of material, specifically prepared to take the junior school reader through an exacting and rigorous course, so that his powers of discrimination and his ability to make a fine use of the text will reach a high pitch of development. In this way the child will be led away from too much concern about words to rely more upon the structure and patterns of language as a vehicle for conveying the infinite variety of meaning.

Comprehension and projects

A different form of exercise in comprehension was to be found in work on projects and topics. Children were required to read information from reference books and reproduce in a certain form this information, which then was placed in a personal or group folder. The idea behind this was threefold: it allowed scope for individual interests; it trained children in the use of books and in the gathering of information; and it trained children to report the information they had collected. In many ways this form of activity produced some excellent results. Interest frequently ran high and much was learnt, but in its usual form it was not a very exacting exercise in comprehension.

The main reason for this was that neither the material to be read nor the reproduction of the information gathered was in any sense controlled. If 'project work' is to be utilized in the reading programme, then it will be necessary to aim at higher standards of achievement in the reports. This can only be achieved if what the children read is presented in a manner which challenges them to think, to discriminate between possible interpretations of the material, to translate it into terms compatible with the terms of reference and format of their reports. Finally, they must be required to evaluate their own report in

61

comparison with other reports and with the original texts. This may sound too difficult for the junior school child, but that is not so. It is all a matter of degree. As the child progresses through the school, this progress will show itself in his work. Bruner (1960) believes that most concepts can be understood by children provided that they are couched in terms suited to the child's stage of mental development. Similarly, it is possible to expect an increasing degree of accomplishment in all manner of things, if they are prepared and pitched at a suitable level.

A further point, in which the usual type of 'project work' is ineffective as an exercise in comprehension, is that the task was usually too wide or general in scope. For example, a child asked to write on Tudor houses would, in all probability, select a particular type or size of house and proceed to describe it. This would rarely involve any form of interpretation on the part of this child; they would simply write their report 'in other words'. Usually they were forced to do this by the text which is, in most books for juniors, merely factual and in no way evaluative, and by the lack of training in the formulation of evaluative criteria. If, on the other hand, the section they read on Tudor houses gave certain facts in such a way that they could be interpreted in terms of, say, building resources, the geographical and social environment, and so on; and if the children were expected, in the upper junior school, to draw some conclusions from this, then there would be comprehension and understanding in the sense of interpretation of text. An attempt to encourage this type of thinking will be found in a series of history books by Coltham and Wright (1967). There is scope in these for the teacher to plan many exercises in interpretation.

However, it should not be supposed that comprehension should deal only with historical matters. Advertising is a fruitful field for the interpretation of meaning, and so is sports reporting. The implications are, however, that more books, on all topics, will have to be written with the express purpose of making the reader think, not merely accept a series of facts. It will then be the task of the teacher to challenge the child to interpret the text in a variety of ways.

Comprehending written language

What has been advocated in this chapter is the need for the achievement of greater dexterity in recognizing words *and* an increasing exactness in the understanding of text. Reading is not merely a mechanical response to symbols, it is a process whereby symbols are interpreted and placed within the wider structure of language. This entails, there- fore, not only a knowledge of the sounds that can be attached to symbols, but an understanding of the signific- ance of these sounds and their order and placement in a sequence, for the derivation of meaning. Such an under- standing is already present in the child, but it is uncon- scious (Vygotsky, 1962). The purpose of the teacher should be to lead the child gradually, over the years he spends in the junior school, to a more conscious utilization of his knowledge of language. For example, it is necessary for the child to become increasingly aware of the finer gradations that can be conveyed by a text. The simple formation, *Where are you going?* can have as many mean- ings as there are words, merely by placing the emphasis on any chosen word out of the four.

Where	are you going?

Where	_are_	you going?

Where are	_you_	going?

Where are you	_go_	ing?

Without the markings that have been superimposed upon these sentences, there is nothing in the graphic signals to indicate the particular implications that should be attached to this question. These can only be derived from an understanding of the meaning of the surrounding and especially the preceding text. The child must come to understand that such variations are possible in the meaning of the sentence, _Where are you going?_ Otherwise its preciseness is missed, and it becomes a very blunt and imprecise instrument of meaning. A conscious realization of the flexibility of such a simple four-word text will help the child to see the flexibility of which English is capable.

Similarly, with the sentence _The man hit the boy._ The child should be brought to a conscious realization of all the implications of this simple statement: that the man performed an action; the action was of a particular kind; that the boy was the recipient of this action. Hence, the sentence could be transformed into _The boy was hit by the man._ (An explanation of transformational generative grammar can be found in Thomas, 1965.)

By the manipulation of words and sentences in this manner—by actively engaging in the construction of symbolized meaning—the child will learn to take a more positive part in the construction and interpretation of language; the aim of the teacher should be to achieve a greater understanding of text through an increasing awareness of the finer gradations of language.

Fries (1952), whilst accepting the fact that individual words have meaning in the dictionary sense, maintains that it is the interpretation of the signs of structural meaning that makes it possible for a text to communicate information in an intelligible form.

Goodman (1963) identifies these signs (or as he calls them, signals) of structural meaning under three headings.

1. Inflectional changes in words: for example, the alteration of the vowel or the addition of *ed* to denote the past tense, and the addition of *es* or *s* or the alteration of the vowel to denote singular or plural. The importance of an awareness of these inflectional changes in spoken English is obvious, for a child can only realize that the written form, *The boy run*, is wrong if, when he speaks the words aloud, they sound wrong.

2. Patterns of word order vary with the intended meaning. *You are coming* can be given a different meaning by rearranging the words to *Are you coming?* Words can change their function by changing their position in relation to other words in the sentence:

> I shop at the Co-op
> The Co-op is a shop
> The Co-op has a shop-boy.

Children in the junior school will gradually learn to use these variations in the order and patterns of words; the teacher's task is to bring about a gradual awareness of their significance in language.

3. Function words or structure words are those words which can be compared with mortar, and are distinguishable from form words which can be compared with bricks.

In the sentence *The boy was hit by the ball*, the function or structure words are *The, was, by, the,* whilst *boy, hit, ball* are form words. The latter provide the substance of the sentence, whilst the former give order to the substance (Thomas, 1965). The function words, in the terms used by the older grammarians, can loosely be taken to include conjunctions, prepositions, auxiliary verbs, definite and indefinite articles. It is by an emerging sophistication in the use of these words and the interpretation of the signals they emit, that the child is able to understand finer and more subtle gradations of meaning.

One of the objectives of the junior school teacher should be to devise a programme of instructions, exercise and discovery, designed to increase gradually the child's ability to interpret these signals. Naturally, this should be introduced over a period of years. There should be no attempt to cram it into a short period of time. Thus, it should not all be left until the final year in the junior school. Neither should it involve too much formal teaching. In many instances the child will experience this awareness if he is brought into positions where he has to use language to achieve his purpose, and is then helped by the teacher to accomplish the task effectively.

Some teachers may be tempted to read into this a call for greater formality in the study of language; a few may even see it as the 'thin edge of a wedge' which would result in a return to the study of grammar. However this is patently not so. The study of language is much wider than the study of grammar, and in this case means a progressive move towards an awareness of the possibilities of language, which can be achieved within the framework of an exciting school environment. The report of the

Plowden Committee, whilst successfully evading the issue by saying that the report *Project English* of the Schools Council will probably have more to say about the study of language, did go so far as to confide that 'Children are interested in words, their shape [whatever that may mean, presumably not pictorial shape!], sound, meaning and origin, and this interest should be exploited in all kinds of incidental ways'. The same report went on to suggest that 'when "rules" or generalizations are discussed these should be "induced" from the child's own knowledge of the usage of the language. The theory of grammar that is studied should describe the child's language and not be a theory based on Latin, many of whose categories, inflexions, case systems, tenses and so on do not exist in English'. Perhaps *Project English* will work it all out in terms of stages of behavioural development. Until this is done, reading as part of language development in the junior school will remain a very haphazard business.

But at least we now know where we should be going. A greater insight into the implications of his reading by the junior school child obviously entails a greater understanding of language. This understanding can only be achieved by manipulating and experimenting with language. Therefore, part of the reading programme for juniors will consist of the construction of text, part will involve the interpretation of other people's text. Reading, language study, writing, are bound closely one to the other.

6

Quicker reading in the junior school

Variable reading

In any programme of reading development in the junior school, some place must be given to quicker reading, which is merely a popular term which covers more effective and efficient reading. There seems no valid reason for trying to make the child think he must read all types of text in the same way or for assuming that the child will automatically realize that he should adjust his speed and ways of reading to suit the text. No adult skilled reader would think of reading a light novel in the same way as he would read a classic, or a classic in the same way as he would read a technical book. Different texts are read for different purposes and in different ways. Even the way in which an adult reads a novel differs according to the text. Some passages can be read quickly and lightly, others are dwelt upon, thought about and savoured. To read every passage in the same way and at the same speed would merely reveal the reader's lack of discrimination. Therefore, why not introduce the child to this idea of variable reading?

Merely telling the children about variable reading, however, would not be enough. It would be necessary to introduce him to situations in which he would have to read for various purposes: sometimes very simple instructions, sometimes detailed instructions; sometimes for lighthearted fun, sometimes for serious meditation. Wherever possible these exercises should be part of a real situation and they should be closely connected with the work of the class.

Similarly, with instruction in how to study a text. It is surprising that so many undergraduates pass through their secondary schools, let alone their primary schools, without any introduction to the various ways of studying. A start could be made in the junior school. Every child uses scanning to some extent, so there is every reason for discussing this technique with him in the hope of extending and perfecting its use as a means of quickly ascertaining the contents of a book. It merely involves reading the table of contents, headings, sub-headings, and the occasional sentence. This will be enough, usually, to tell the reader whether there is a high probability that the book contains what he is looking for. Skipping is another device, frequently used with a sense of guilt. The reader omits everything that is not absolutely pertinent to his requirements. Sometimes it will mean the omission of chapters and sometimes merely paragraphs or sentences, but what is the use of reading the parts of a book that are irrelevant to the needs of the reader at that moment. For example, there is little to be gained in the normal way from reading about Dewey when collecting Plato's ideas on education. So much work has to be done under pressure, that it is impossible to digress into numerous allied fields.

Skimming

Skimming falls into a different category. Children and many adults are generally very inept at this, probably through a dogmatic and rigid insistence upon a left to right sequence at all times when reading. Therefore the introduction of skimming rests entirely with the teacher. The basis of skimming procedure is the reader's familiarity with the constraints of language. Because these are severe in many instances, the reader can, by picking up significant words here and there, anticipate the intervening words without bothering to perceive them, and still obtain the sense of the text. Naturally, the more familiar the reader is with the constraints of written language, the easier it will be for him to skim effectively. Hence the importance of some sort of programme for the development of language facility. Skimming is not an easy thing to do. It requires practice and the application of some intelligence. Any programme in the development of the skill of skimming should be very gradual indeed. The crash course in quicker reading for adults has no place as such in the junior school. A start can be made with the simple use of flash cards containing phrases and very short sentences, containing one highly significant and suggestive word. Over the years the length of the text flashed will be increased, but care should be taken never to out-pace the child to any marked extent, otherwise a loss of confidence will cause serious regression. Various other devices could be used, such as cards of instructions to be read very quickly and acted upon.

SQ3R

In the fourth year of the junior school, the normal reader could be introduced to the SQ3R method of study. The child *scans* the book or shorter text which he is about to study, and as he scans he formulates what he considers to be the most important *questions* he would hope to have answered by reading the book. Having written these questions down, the child *reads* (1R) the text and then tries to *recall* (2R) the answers to his questions, and checks these with the text. Later, possibly some days later, the child should *revise* (3R) what he has learnt by rereading the text and rewriting the answers to his questions. The answers he writes should be in the form of notes and the important parts should be denoted by underlining and other forms of marking (McLaughlin and Coles, 1966).

This is one method of studying a text. Other methods, which are less comprehensive and easier to employ by the younger children, could be worked out to suit the different stages in the junior school.

As for specific training in more rapid reading, it seems questionable whether the junior school is the appropriate place to introduce such a specialized form of instruction. If the other parts of the reading programme are effectively carried out, and if the reading material is sufficiently interesting and varied in its content, there seems good reason to believe that the children will automatically increase their speed of reading.

7

A method to meet the needs of backward readers

Causes of backwardness

Many teachers of nine-, ten- and eleven-year-old backward readers have difficulty in finding a method which will help these children to forget their failure and restart the process of learning to read with ease and fluency. They will, of course, be aware of the fact that the backwardness may be caused by physical defects in sight or hearing, or by emotional disturbance (Vernon, 1957), and the teacher should examine these possibilities by obtaining advice from the educational psychologist and using, with care, diagnostic tests and observations. However, it is not the purpose of this chapter to examine testing or to prescribe methods for children with physical or emotional defects. There are many backward readers who, for one reason or another, have just not mastered the difficulties of reading. They have no physical defects which should impede their progress in reading and the degree of emotional disturbance does not appear to be sufficient to cause them any insuperable difficulties. To all outward appearances they are just slower children.

It may be that the methods employed when they were first introduced to reading were unsuitable or they may have failed to master crucial parts of their training in the basic reading skills. Dr Joyce Morris (1966) found some of the following deficiencies amongst poor readers: inability to tackle isolated words, insufficient knowledge of the names and sounds of the letters of the alphabet, limited ability in the analysis and synthesis of words in terms of their constituent sounds, lack of directional attack upon words, inattention to the details of words, and inadequate capacity to memorize words. Birch and Belmont (1964) have suggested that one of the difficulties retarded readers experience is that of integrating what is seen with the appropriate sounds. Blank and Bridger (1966) accept this finding, but they suggest that it may be more exactly explained by a failure to label the letters of a word. They do not exclude other explanations; for example, that retarded readers possess a knowledge of the labels but do not use them because they pay insufficient attention to detail, or that there may be a defect in the sensory systems. However, the important implication of these researches for classroom procedure is that a remedial method in general use should be one which emphasizes and helps both the application of the relevant verbal labels to the visually presented words and letters, and also the integration of auditory-visual information. In doing this it may enable the children to learn to accomplish those parts of the skill that they have missed.

Of course there may be other factors which have played their part. These children may not have been sufficiently interested in the content of the reading materials and lessons to want to learn to read; they may not have been compatible with their teacher; or there may have been any one or more of a number of influences working upon them in such a way as to distract them from reading— for example, home circumstances, where there was a lack of respect for reading. Any one of these factors could have prevented the child from concentrating upon learning to read at a vital stage and, thereby, he could have missed crucial parts of the instructional programme.

Requirements of the teacher

The teacher, in these circumstances, requires a method which rekindles the child's desire to read and enables that child to retrieve the situation by learning what he may have missed. It is not a clinical situation where one teacher is able to deal with one child. On the contrary, there are thirty to forty children in the class and, therefore, the method chosen must be comprehensive, even though, as in the case of unstreamed classes, the number of children requiring remedial teaching may be half-a-dozen at the most. In more homogeneous classes this number will be substantially higher. In these situations the main method or approach must provide a comprehensive coverage of a large number of possible deficiencies in reading and, at the same time, it must be simple to operate and control.

Fernald's method

One method which is sometimes suggested is that described and used by Grace Fernald (1943). Unfortunately, most of those who advocate this method stipulate that it is good 'as a last resort'. Why, it is difficult to understand, unless it is because it involves the teacher in a little extra unusual work! But then surely some deviation from normal practice is absolutely essential if children have reached the age of nine or ten and are still finding reading difficult. And most teachers, in charge of children in such dire circumstances, are only too pleased to adopt any method which may succeed. Fernald's method, described in chapter five of her book and designated as a method for total or extreme disability, has all the ingredients of a general and valid method of remedial teaching.

The needs of the children

When studying a remedial method for teaching children to read, it is important that the first consideration should be the general needs of the children. It must be remembered that <u>these children have failed and that they know that they have failed</u>. This creates a situation so critical that any feasible method must create the conditions in which learning will again be possible. In order to accomplish this, five general needs must be covered. They are:

1. <u>The children need to be convinced that they can learn.</u>

2. They need to be shown a mechanical process which will help them to learn and remember words and phrases and which gives them an insight into how words are constructed.

3. They need a totally different method of learning to read.

4. They need something which shows clearly and instantly any progress they make.

5. They may need specific help in certain aspects of reading.

Having defined the needs of the children and their requirements in broad terms of methodology, it is now possible to examine Fernald's method in detail and to see how it fulfils these needs.

The first and second needs

The first and imperative need is what Fernald called reconditioning: the teacher must convince the children that they can learn, that their failure up to now has not been their fault but rather the fault of the methods by which they have been taught previously. And to lighten the whole aspect of their expectation of the new burden about to be thrust upon them, they can be told that all that has been lacking is that they have not been shown the 'tricks of the trade' and that now they are about to be introduced to the secrets; everyone knows the strength of the human desire to belong to an 'in-group'!

This leads to the second need. It is useless to tell these children to learn words or phrases without showing them how to set about learning. They need some framework of active participation in the learning process, which is mechanical and remains constant. It should also be capable of easy adaptation at later stages as the child progresses.

When one examines the details of the ways in which Fernald's method deals with these two needs, one sees that she spared no effort during the reconditioning period to convince the children that they could learn words. A reputedly retarded reader is asked to choose a word he thinks is difficult. This word is then written in large writing on a piece of paper and the child traces over the word with his forefinger. Simultaneously, he pronounces the syllables of the word, e.g. pen-cil.

The tracing and vocalization of the word are repeated, ten or twenty times, until the child thinks that he can write the word without copying. When he has tested himself on another piece of paper, and is satisfied that he knows the details of the word, he is asked to display his ability to the class by writing the word unaided on the blackboard. The effect of success on the child, and on the rest of the class is electrifying. All are keen to try this 'new trick'.

Failure by any child to write the word correctly can be redeemed by the teacher striking an optimistic attitude and asking the child to continue the tracing and vocalization a little longer. At this stage it is imperative that success is achieved, even if the child has to trace the word fifty times in all.

This method of learning new words is simple, direct, and whilst conforming to a single pattern which a teacher can impose upon a large number of children, it incorporates a wide variety of ways of learning words, by visual, auditory, tactile and kinaesthetic means. As such, it is extremely useful for the teacher who knows little of the sophisticated ways of dealing with backwardness in reading, but who, nevertheless, has to face every day a class of children who desperately need help. The child's 'attention is not called to the words he does not know but to the fact that he is capable of learning any words he wants to learn' (Fernald). Furthermore, it seems reasonable to suppose that by constantly tracing and saying the parts of words, the child will gain an understanding of the construction of words. This knowledge will call the child's attention to the integration of visual stimuli and auditory responses and it will help him to make the predictions about clusters of letters, which Gibson (1963) found so important.

One note of caution should be introduced. It is absolutely essential to the whole of Fernald's method that the tracing should be done on the paper with the fore-finger. Neither a pencil nor tracing paper should be used, for these impede learning through the tactile and kinaesthetic senses. Even adults find it difficult to copy letters, or anything else, through tracing paper. The con-centrated effort that is necessary to hold the tracing paper in place and to follow the lines of the letters, divert the child's attention from the general kinaesthetic 'feel' of the word—i.e. the rhythmical movement involved in tracing the word with a finger. The experiment of Miles (1928) and Husband (1928) and Fernald's own comments show the advantages of direct unimpeded contact between paper and finger as a learning device.

N. B.

The third and fourth needs

The third need is for something totally different from any-thing that they have had in the past. It should be a method or device which is within their ken, in that they can manipulate it with ease; it must hold their attention through manipulation; and it must, by its approach, hold their interest. It must, in effect, be something which gets away from the type of books on which they have failed and from the apparatus and all the paraphernalia of post infant school doldrums, into which these children may have been cast.

Yet they need something which shows clearly and instantly any progress they make, and which constantly reminds them that they are making progress in reading—not in games, not in exercises, but in actually reading the written text.

Fernald's method gives them something totally different.

78

It does not rely upon reading books (although it certainly does not exclude them) and it does not require any apparatus apart from pencil and paper. It is based upon the construction of their own reading material by the children. Once they have been reconditioned and introduced to the tracing-vocalization method of learning words, they are asked to write stories which will be placed, eventually, in their own 'reading book'. These stories can be written about any topic and can be of any length, from one sentence to as many pages as the pupil or teacher likes. Any words they cannot spell are written for them by the teacher and are learnt by the tracing-vocalization method before being used in the story. A record of these words is kept in a personal box file by each child. (The cardboard boxes which contain Cadbury's penny and twopenny bars of chocolate are entirely satisfactory for this purpose.) Other teachers may prefer to keep a record of these words by writing them on the back of the child's original story, storing them, and periodically handing them back to the child for him to revise the words he has learnt. Both these ways of recording new words have their advantages. The former is neater, it forms an easy means of reference back to words already learnt, and it acquaints the child with alphabetical order. The latter is by no means an easy form for referring back, but for the purposes of revision it enables the child to re-encounter all these words within the meaningful and perhaps vivid setting in which they were first encountered. Meaningful associations would be rekindled and the child's facility in their usage would be enhanced.

When the story is completed the teacher reprints it, with reasonable corrections to grammar and without any spelling mistakes, within twenty-four hours, if possible;

it is pasted into the child's 'reading book' and the child reads it aloud to the teacher.

As time goes on the tracing and vocalization may diminish and gradually disappear, so that the child is then left with a method of learning words which has evolved out of the tracing and vocalization and which is satisfactory to the child.

The advantages of this form of reading lesson are obvious. It is different, it is simple, and it is relevant to reading because it leads the child on, not only to reading, but to the construction of a book which he and others can read. The child is working to some purpose, he gains a sense of creative achievement, his interest is held by the objectives of the task and his concentration is ensured by the mechanical nature of the task. How often do we hear teachers complain 'If only he could concentrate for long enough'. Fernald's method is a constructive answer to this plea.

As the 'reading book' grows, so does the confidence of the child, for he is now able to give demonstrative proof of what he has always hoped was the case, namely that he can remember how to read what he has written. He can even secretly test his powers of transfer by trying to read some other reading book that is left lying around. And so his confidence grows visibly and quickly. Likewise, his understanding of the construction of written language grows. He learns to translate spoken into written language and to express his thoughts and ideas with increasing facility, and in doing so, he increases his understanding of language, especially written language, and thereby increases his ability to interpret other people's writing.

In Chapter Six of her book, entitled 'Partial Disability', Fernald sets out her suggestions for the next stage, when the child passes on to read printed books. She suggests that the child should scan the current paragraph or page for unknown words before attempting to read it. These he lightly underlines and the teacher pronounces them for him. The child then learns the word, either by tracing and vocalization or by some other suitable method, and finally writes it without copying. Then he reads the text.

An adaptation of this procedure, which may be easier OR to operate in a large class, is one in which the child asks the teacher for help with any unknown words as they occur during the actual reading of text. The teacher merely pronounces the word for the child and writes it on a slip of paper. The child then continues reading, but, at a convenient place to break the reading, for example, the end of a chapter or story, the child learns these words in the way suggested by Fernald. The slips of paper containing the words which the child has learnt are retained for reference and revision. A box file of all new words can be compiled.

The fifth need

Finally, the type of child with whom this chapter has been concerned may need specific help in certain aspects of reading or at certain stages in his progress. For example, he may find the irregularities of grapheme-phoneme correspondence disconcerting and the phonic conventions bewildering. Stott's *Programmed Reading Kit*, the appropriate *S.R.A. Reading Laboratory*, some of the games and exercises from *Fun with Phonics* and *Sounds and Words*, or Monroe's emphasis on defining and dealing with specific deficiencies, all have something to offer, and the teacher should easily find enough here to supplement the Fernald method. But it is possible that children who are backward in reading, but who do not suffer from physical defects or severe emotional disturbances, may need specific help outside the normally accepted scope of reading schemes. They may need applied speech training to obliterate or compensate for irregularities in speech which distort the auditory interpretation of written symbols, or they may need to be brought to a clearer awareness of the meaning of language, through an understanding of the significance of stress, intonation and sentence patterns. Much can be done to imbue the text with life, individuality, significance and meaning, if children are shown how radically the meaning of passages can be altered merely by changing the manner in which they are read.

The importance of Fernald's method

Before leaving the contribution of Fernald to the alleviation of reading difficulty, it would emphasize the importance of her ideas if the reason for the success of her method were evaluated. Perhaps the most important factor is the motivational one. Her method is basically a language-experience approach, but in its purest form—in that all the words read come directly from the child. This being the case, everything the child is asked to read is based upon his own experience or interest, and the whole edifice of learning is built upon familiarity.

As far as word recognition is concerned there are three advantages. It seems probable that this method helps the child to blend letter sounds by specifically training him in this procedure. This is particularly important, because, as Jeanne Chall (1963) found, ability to blend letter sounds is closely related to reading ability. In the second place, young children and retarded readers have some difficulty in associating visually and auditorily perceived patterns (Birch and Belmont, 1964 and 1965). In this case it seems probable that Fernald's method aids children to make this association.

Order and orientation of letters and sounds frequently are another source of difficulty in the early stages of reading (Vernon, 1957). Fernald's method imposes a systematic left to right orientation and causes the child to note the order of grapheme-phoneme correspondences.

Finally, an advantage of this method is that it combines reading and writing and it incorporates spelling. Therefore it can form, for those children who need it, a major part of the work in English. The writing of stories replaces the more usual types of written English lesson, instruction in spelling is catered for; and the teacher, although he has to rewrite the stories for the children, is released from the marking of essays and other written work. Some teachers have, in the past, been deterred by the prospect of stories to be rewritten piling up, but surely it is up to the individual teacher to control the number of stories written under this scheme. Perhaps one of its most useful characteristics is that this method can be used to whatever degree thought necessary by the teacher. It can be used with small or large groups and it can be used periodically as an alternative to other types of reading lesson, without conflicting with them.

Other considerations

This chapter has dealt with one method of teaching children to read at an age which is later than normal. It does not pretend to answer all the problems of backwardness in reading. All it suggests is that with some children, who are finding reading difficult, some degree of success will be achieved by engaging them in tasks, the performance of which will give them some insight into the nature of written language and its interpretation.

There have been some recent researches by Collins (1961) Lovell and others (1963) which may lead us to question some aspects of the long-term effectiveness of remedial teaching. It is imperative that all teachers who are in contact with children who have received some form of remedial teaching should not make the mistake of believing that once the child has begun to read with some fluency his troubles are over. This is obviously not so. There is no reason, that we know of so far, to suppose that having mastered the simpler sub-skills of reading he will find the later sub-skills, such as items 12 and 13 in the list given in Chapter Three, within easy attainment. Indeed, the fact that he was slow to master the former should indicate that he may be slow to master the latter. Furthermore, just as it has been stressed that normal readers need a continuing programme of help throughout the stages when they are perfecting their already achieved reading skill, so backward readers will need such help and guidance in greater measure. It follows then, that if a child requires remedial teaching in the upper junior school, he also requires a programme of remedial instruction in the lower secondary school at least. This will be necessary no matter how great the improvement he made in the upper junior school, for even where this improvement is substantial, a programme designed to increase his ability in reading, as distinct from a programme designed to teach him to read, will be necessary. Once it has been found that a child has difficulty in learning to read, that child should

84

be kept under close but discreet surveillance for several years after the initial remedial work has been undertaken, and the work that he does in school should be planned accordingly.

8

The task of the teacher

Diversity

It is very difficult to define the task of the teacher,
especially in a system of education such as exists in
Britain. Each school is free to determine the methods by
which it will teach its pupils to read, and in many cases
individual teachers within the school will vary in the
methods they use. The result is that for one term a child
may be with a teacher who emphasizes a phonic method,
and the next term find himself with a teacher who bases
her teaching upon a word-whole, look-and-say method.
There may also be variation in the more general approach
to teaching and learning: emphasis may be given to
systematic teaching in one school or class, and to
incidental learning in another.

But the difficulty in defining the task of the teacher
does not end there. Differences between the reading
problems at different stages cause this task to vary
accordingly. Sometimes the variations will be slight, yet
at other times they will be of considerable magnitude.
This is particularly so when one considers the difference
between reading problems in the infant school and those
in the junior school. In the infant school, the basic problem
is likely to derive from the difficulty, on the part of the

child, in understanding how to learn the skill of reading and translate it into the interpretation of the language signals of the text. This may lead to untold bewilderment in the mind of the child. Lack of motivation in this case will stem, not from frustration at past failure, but from a failure to see and understand the purpose of the whole process of reading.

In the junior school the problems are more likely to centre on a sense of failure in those who are failing to read. As the child becomes more conscious of his failure to learn to read, his feelings of frustration increase and he is reluctant to read, not because he is lacking in a desire to learn but because he is concerned not to attempt something at which he has already experienced failure. No child can stand continuous failure.

Of course, there are other problems which arise in the junior school, which are not connected with backwardness in reading. It is only now being realized that the teaching of reading should not stop as soon as the child can read simple text. Dr Joyce Morris, and many Americans, have been stressing for some time the need to think out what should be done to increase reading skill beyond the stage at which teaching usually finishes—the end of the infant school in the case of many children who are succeeding in reading. This will present teachers in the junior school with many problems which have hardly been defined, let alone tackled.

The teacher in the infant school

Obviously, the task of the teacher will vary according to the problems with which she is faced. In the infant school, in addition to a rich programme of pre-reading

87

experience and general language development, the teaching will be concerned with the learning of the sub-skills and the interpretation of meaning from written symbols. The teacher will usually find it easy to arouse the child's confidence, but her main problem will be to see that it is not destroyed. Once a child's confidence, at the infant stage, is destroyed, the child and the teacher face serious difficulty. The teacher has to strike a balance between instruction and practice—there must be enough instruction to give the child the necessary ability and confidence to succeed in the practice. This will vary from task to task and from child to child and, therefore, it is very critical in application. No one can dogmatically prescribe how much instruction is necessary; only the teacher is in a position to make the assessment of the factors involved. All that can be said is, surely we wish to preserve for the child as much time for independent action on his part as possible. As the type of lesson varies, from instruction to practice or experimentation, the task of the teacher will vary between that of instructor and that of guide or adviser, or even that of an inspirer to fresh action.

The teacher in the junior school

In the junior school, the teacher of backward readers will be faced with a very different situation. Here the first concern will be to restore the confidence of these children in their ability to learn. There must be a period of re-conditioning and re-motivation. Only after this has been done can any progress be made in teaching the children to read. Whereas the infant teacher usually begins with children who have had little done to destroy their confidence in learning to read, the teacher of backward readers in the junior school begins with children who have little or no confidence. However, once confidence has been restored, the older child is capable of taking a greater and increasing responsibility for his own learning. It is vitally important that this responsibility should be granted, because it will help to strengthen the child's confidence. One thing should be avoided at all costs: neither the teaching methods nor the materials should resemble those which are normally connected with the teaching of reading in the infant school. This in particular applies to reading books. To teach the nine-year-old in ways that faintly resemble those employed with seven-year-olds is merely to heap indignity upon disappointment at failure.

Many people have been amazed by stories of adult convicts being taught to read by infant methods, but this is an entirely different matter. In these cases the motive for learning to read is so strong and runs so deep that the student is prepared to submit to any means in order to achieve the desired end. Fortunately, seldom does one find a child in the junior school who has reached such a fearful state.

A crash course

Perhaps the best way to tackle the problem of backward readers in the upper junior school is to institute a crash course, which would involve the child in some form of reading activity during several short periods each day. This would have the effect of getting the children to a stage in a very short time where their progress is obvious, even to themselves, and so would form an intrinsic part in the development of self-confidence. The teacher's task in these circumstances is a highly critical one. There must be some form of constant drive, but it must never exceed the limits which would destroy confidence. Firmness is required, because from this the child will be imbued with some of the confidence which lies behind it. A teacher who is firm, knows he is going to achieve a particular end; and if a sympathetic approach to the child is mixed with this firmness, then the child will soon realize that the teacher is working for and with him, rather than against him. Determination should be an essential part of the teacher's mental equipment, and then, provided that he knows something of the subject matter—although unfortunately this cannot always be taken for granted—he will place the child in the favourable learning situation of *expecting* to learn something. Too many backward children in our junior schools are placed in the position of not really expecting, or being expected, to make any substantial progress in learning. Much of the work is so arranged that it merely proves over and over again to the child how little he knows, rather than showing him how much he is capable of learning.

Naturally it is very difficult always to pitch the work at the required level, and occasionally things will go wrong; but it is part of the task of the teacher to be aware of this possibility. If he is aware of this, then he will be in a better position to forestall failure and ensure a generally, although not an invariably, rising pattern of success.

Flexibility and self-criticism

Whatever methods the teacher of reading at every stage may use, it is vital to her effectiveness as a teacher that she should be continuously reassessing the part she plays in every phase of her work. She should, after every reading period, say to herself, 'Given that type of situation, how effectively did I perform my task?' Only by doing this will a teacher make any significant improvements in her teaching. All the extra in-service courses will be of no avail if this question is not asked and an attempt made to answer it—for it implies that thought has gone into the planning and preparation of every lesson and that she is prepared to alter her teaching techniques as a result of self-criticism.

In conclusion, it must be reiterated that so much depends upon the teacher. No matter what approach is used, across the whole span from formal to informal techniques, the part played by the teacher is crucial. Nothing can replace efficient and inspiring teaching. Dr. Joyce Morris (1966), reporting her researches in many schools in Kent, strongly supports this when she suggests that 'the actual reading methods used appeared to matter far less than the manner and skill with which they were employed, and other attributes of the teachers concerned'. In fact, it is the implementation and manipulation of the methods that are the vital factors. Methods, in themselves, can achieve very little.

9

Training students

Many people have expressed concern recently that students in colleges of education and university departments of education are not receiving an adequate amount of instruction in the ways and methods of teaching children to read. It is not the intention of this book to decide whether this concern is justified. Some enquiries made in colleges of education in the north west of England revealed that in all colleges in that area students received help and instruction in the teaching of reading. The amount and type of training varied from college to college, but the encouraging thing that emerged from these enquiries was that something was being done about the teaching of reading. Whether or not this is general throughout the country it is impossible to say without further enquiries. However, it is possible to examine some of the difficulties which arise in the training of students to teach children how to read and then to suggest tentatively what is and what is not possible in the course of training.

The student and reading

The difficulties are really forbidding in their complexity. The normal student is usually a person who finds reading both easy and pleasurable. It is unlikely that he has experienced any difficulty in learning to read, and he has probably received every encouragement to utilize fully his skill at all stages of his development. Therefore, unlike mathematics (for instance), where he may well have experienced difficulties at many stages, including recent ones at the secondary stage, in reading he will be almost totally unaware of the difficulties that can face a child in the early stages of learning. This lack of personal experience in the difficulties of learning to read is further aggravated by a lack of understanding of the reading process as such. He will, in all probability, have no conception of the constituent parts of the reading process— what constitutes reading, what is involved in the skill of reading—and, therefore, he will be unable to foresee the difficulties with which the child learner is faced. This is the foremost problem of the student. It means that not only does he have difficulty in understanding the essence of reading, but also that he will be unable to classify and categorize the difficulties when he actually meets them. For example, in a case where a child cannot synthesize the phonemes of a word, the student may be unable to ascertain that it is this that is causing the difficulty. He almost certainly will not know all the implications of this difficulty and, therefore, he will be less capable of helping the child than a teacher who is able to pinpoint this particular difficulty. Furthermore, he will have no readily available store of methods and techniques for dealing with these difficulties, even if he can identify them. He will not know Fernald's trick for distinguishing between *b* and *d*—drawing a bed in outline ⊢⊣ and then filling in the letters **bed** —or her way of countering mirror writing, and so on.

These problems form the basic difficulties of the student at the outset of his training. There are others which are no less formidable, although different in nature. The student lacks the organizational powers of the skilled teacher. He may know that a group of children is facing difficulties in reading; he may even understand these difficulties and have some ideas on how to rectify matters; but his over-riding problem may well be how to organize the class in order to allow himself the freedom to deal with that group or individual. He may find all sorts of obstacles to face : not only how to organize the rest of the class, but how to arrange the work of the group which is finding difficulty, so that he can achieve his objectives within the particular time available. The reading difficulties may be more acute in some children in the group than in others. And there are other problems, depending upon the particular circumstances.

The shortness of the period of school practice only allows the student time to deal with a very small section in any programme or scheme for teaching children to read. He will not be able to see the whole process nor even a substantial part of it. Therefore he will have to enter full-time teaching with very little practical experience of teaching children to read and with substantial parts of the process untouched. This is certainly not realized by those head teachers who expect their probationary teachers to teach children to read with some degree of skill.

Another result of the shortage of time available for the theoretical and practical study of the teaching of reading is that students and probationary teachers are frequently unable to see all the implications of the schemes of work which the school is using. It is possible to study only a small selection of the reading schemes in use in schools in this country, and if the student or inexperienced teacher is faced by one of those schemes not selected for study during his period of training, he will find it very difficult, if not impossible, to use the scheme effectively at the outset.

It is very easy for people who have devoted a great portion of their lives to the teaching of reading or who find a particular interest in it, to forget that on top of all this the student has many other problems to contend with in teaching other subjects.

Plan of the initial course

With these limitations in mind it is a useful exercise to attempt to establish some form of plan to give a student the maximum help within these rather formidable limitations. Such a plan can only be very general in nature. Much will depend upon the abilities of the student and the lecturer.

It is fairly obvious from all that has been written in the earlier chapters that the first thing to do is to try to establish what is involved in skilled reading. Only by doing this at the outset will a student be able to comprehend the nature of reading. From this, it might be a useful exercise to extract possible points of difficulty facing the learner and the less skilful reader.

Once the student has some idea of what is involved in skilled reading, it will then be possible to establish roughly what has to be learnt. This will bring the student face to face with the sub-skills of reading. Alongside this, it will be necessary for the student to gain some idea of the ways in which learning takes place. He will need to become acquainted with learning theory, and it will be necessary to attempt to apply this to the learning of the sub-skills: how an attempt can be made to teach the grapheme-phoneme correspondences, the sequences of letters and sounds, the digraphs, the strings of letters, words, and so on. The student will know from his examination of skilled reading that reading is a matter of interpreting the text. What can he do to help the child to interpret words, strings of words, paragraphs and complete passages?

These three elements—a study of skilled reading, the identification of the skills to be learnt and ways of teaching these skills—form the basic and essential features in the student's training. Without these all will be meaningless, and the student will be left groping, as so many have been in the past, not knowing what to do or what method to use, and easy prey for any unthinking enthusiast to thrust his favoured method upon someone quite different in temperament, personality and ability as a teacher.

When these three elements have been adequately dealt with, it will then be possible to consider with some degree of detachment and discrimination the various general methods of teaching children to read which have been used in the past: the alphabetic method, the early phonic methods, look-and-say, and the more sophisticated phonic 'whole-word' methods that are emerging today. A consideration of the influence of the study of linguistics is apposite here, and it will give an air of reality to the study of these methods if two or three published schemes of teaching children to read are examined critically and in some detail. A possible balanced selection would be *The Janet and John Reading Scheme*, both phonic and look-and-say series, *The Royal Road Readers*, and *The Queensway Readers*. This would give the student a more intimate insight into the practical side of the phonic and look-and-say methods and it would enable a critical review of basic reading books.

Practical work

It will also be necessary to deal with the organizational aspects of a reading lesson. On the first and second periods of school practice, assuming these to be approximately eight to ten weeks in all, it would dovetail neatly with the above proposed introduction to the teaching of reading, if each student concentrated upon a small group of three or four children. By doing this the student would be able to work out in detail some particular aspect of learning to read. He would be able to study in some depth the child's reactions to a problem, and he would be able to work out and apply some teaching responses to the case in question. It would not be possible to do this if, simultaneously, the student had to be responsible for the whole class. His attention would be diverted and he would not be able to give sufficient attention to detail. At about the same time as this practical work, there should be theoretical discussion between student and tutor, and teacher and other students where possible, which centre upon the practical problems.

The third or final practice will be different. Here it will be necessary for the student to attempt to give his attention to small groups and to individuals whilst controlling the whole class. This means that his organizational problems will be increased. Now, it will be not merely a question of what needs to be done and how to do it, but how to fit this in with all the other things to be done with the remainder of the class. Naturally, too much cannot be expected in these circumstances. Nevertheless, the student has to be introduced to the realities of a school school teaching situation, where classes are usually in the thirties and forties and seldom is there any auxiliary help available.

Many students find the organizational aspect perplexing, and although school practice time should be one of experimentation in teaching techniques, it is not in reality always feasible for the insecure student to vary his organization of the class and its work. He will need much encouragement and help from the tutor. There seems little to be gained by the tutor taking over halfway through a lesson, in order to demonstrate how he would do it. That is not the problem in hand; the problem is how can the *student* do it. Also, the tutor's interruption has the opposite effect to that of showing the student how it should be done; it merely demonstrates to the student something that he probably knows already—that he is making a mess of things. In addition it tends to usurp his authority and undermine his confidence so that he is unable to benefit from his tutor's display of expertise. It would seem far more effective to approach this problem on a level of equality rather than on the basis of teacher and pupil, and to discuss the implications of the situation with the student. Most students have the ability to understand a verbal analysis of a classroom situation. It would be far better to do this and to arrange for them to see, at some other time, skilful practitioners in action—a demonstration by a good teacher with his own class—with the tutor present. He can then direct the ensuing discussion of the demonstration lesson in order to suit the needs of the students and emphasize the significant features of the lesson.

Teaching backward children

When the student has gained some knowledge of the ways of teaching children who have few difficulties in learning to read, he should then be given some idea of the problems of teaching children who are backward in reading. But this should be subsidiary to learning to teach normal children to read. It is very easy to confuse the student at this stage in his training, and teaching backward readers is such a skilled operation that students cannot be expected to become efficient teachers of backward children during the initial training period. Little more can be done than to introduce the student to some basic considerations and to show him a few of the techniques employed in the treatment of backwardness in reading. It is important not to forget that the initial training period can only be an introduction to teaching; it cannot be a full and complete professional apprenticeship and training. The essential thing is to encourage and help the student to think effectively about the problems of teaching.

10

Sources of books for children

It has been estimated by a person with a deep knowledge of children's reading habits that a one-stream entry primary school needs at least 2,000 books, apart from those that can be classed as text books, to cover the wide range of interests that these children will have. This number, it should be emphasized, is an absolute minimum, and any school which has any desire at all to promote a literate and cultured society would undoubtedly aim at a figure far in excess of this.

The difficulty, however, which faces many head teachers, is where to find suitable books. Fortunately, there are now appearing various publications which give lists of books suitable in style and content for primary school children. Naturally, to draw up a complete list would be an impossible task. One way in which teachers and head teachers can see and examine some of the best books for children is by asking the Department of Education and Science to send their exhibition of books, known as the Tann Collection, to their area. This is a particularly fine collection of books, selected with great discrimination by members of the inspectorate. Approaches can be made through the local education authority or through members of H.M.I. It is an opportunity which should not be missed

The Department of Education and Science publish a

pamphlet entitled *Sources of Information about Books and Libraries in Primary and Secondary Schools* (1967). This pamphlet gives sources such as the Bristol University Institute of Education survey of books for backward readers (1956 and 1962), Margery Fisher's book *Intent upon Reading* in which 1,400 books are mentioned, and many others which will help in the selection of books. It also contains a list of books which deal with the formation and organization of school libraries. For example, the Department of Education and Science publications *The School Library* (1967) and *The Use of Books* (1964), and the School Library Association booklet *Using Books in the Primary School* (1966).

A very useful pamphlet, *Using Books and Libraries in Primary Schools*, can be obtained from H. K. Evans, Maes-yr-Haf, 50 Sketty Road, Swansea. Joan Cass (1967) gives a useful book list in her recent book, *Literature and the Young Child*, and so do Obrist and Pickard in the Teacher's Manual to their reading scheme, *Time for Reading*. Finally, no school library could even contemplate being without all the Young Puffin and Puffin Books, published by Penguin, and the Collie Book Series for children up to eight years of age.

Bibliography

ANDERSON, J. E. (1954), 'Methods of Child Psychology', in Carmichael, L. (ed.), *Manual of Child Psychology*, New York: Wiley.

ANDERSON, I. H. and DEARBOARN, W. F. (1952), *The Psychology of Teaching Reading*, New York: Ronald Press.

BARTLETT, F. C. (1947), 'The Measurement of Human Skill', in *British Medical Journal*, Nos 4510 and 4511.

BEREITER, C. and ENGELMANN, S. (1966), *Teaching Disadvantaged Children in the Preschool*, New Jersey: Prentice-Hall.

BERNSTEIN, B. (1960), 'Language and Social Class', in *British Journal of Sociology*, *11*, pp. 271-276.

BERNSTEIN, B. (1961), 'Social Structure, Language and Learning', in *J. Educ. Res.*, *3*, pp. 163-176.

BIRCH, H. G. and BELMONT, L. (1964), 'Auditory-Visual Integration in Normal and Retarded Readers', in *American Journal of Orthopsychiatry*, *34*, pp. 853-861.

BIRCH, H. G. and BELMONT, L. (1965), 'Auditory-Visual Integration, Intelligence and Reading Ability in School Children', in *Perceptual and Motor Skills*, *20*, pp. 295-305.

BLANK, M. and BRIDGER, W. H. (1966), 'Deficiencies in Verbal Labelling in Retarded Readers', in *American Journal of Orthopsychiatry*, *36*, pp. 840-847.

BLOOMFIELD, L. and BARNHART, C. L. (1961), *Let's Read: A Linguistic Approach*, Detroit: Wayne State U.P.

BREARLEY, M. and NEILSON, L. (1964), *Queensway Reading*, London: Evans.

BRISTOL UNIVERSITY, Inst. of Education (1956), *A Survey of Books for Backward Readers*, London: University of London Press.

BIBLIOGRAPHY

BRISTOL UNIVERSITY, Inst. of Education (1962), *A Second Survey of Books for Backward Readers*, London: University of London Press.

BRUCE, D. J. (1964), 'The Analysis of Word Sounds by Young Children', in *British Journal of Educational Psychology*, 34, pp. 158-169.

BRUNER, J. S. (1960), *The Process of Education*, Cambridge: Harvard University Press.

CARVER, C. and STOWASSER, C. H. (1963), *Oxford Colour Reading Books*, Oxford: Oxford University Press.

CASS, J. E. (1967), *Literature and the Young Child*, London: Longmans.

CHALL, J. (1967), *Learning to Read: The Great Debate*, New York: McGraw Hill.

CHALL, J., ROSWELL, F. G. and BLUMENTHAL, S. H. (November 1963), 'Auditory Blending Ability: a Factor in Success in Beginning Reading', in *The Reading Teacher*.

COLLINS, J. W. (1961), 'The Effects of Remedial Education', in *Educational Monographs, IV*. University of Birmingham, Institute of Education.

COLTHAM, J. B. and WRIGHT, W. H. (1967), *Life Then, Norman Times*, London: Hart-Davis.

COLWELL, E. (ed.) (1967), *Time for a Story*. Harmondsworth: Penguin (Young Puffin).

DANIELS, J. C. (1966), 'The Place of Phonics', in Downing, J. (ed.) *The First International Reading Symposium, Oxford, 1964*, London: Cassell.

DANIELS, J. C. and DIACK, H. (1960), *Progress in Reading in the Infant School*, Nottingham: Institute of Education.

DANIELS, J. C. and DIACK, H. (1960), *The Royal Road Readers*, London: Chatto & Windus.

DEPARTMENT OF EDUCATION AND SCIENCE (1964), *The Use of Books*, H.M.S.O.

DEPARTMENT OF EDUCATION AND SCIENCE (1967), *The School Library*, H.M.S.O.

DIACK, H. (1960), *Reading and the Psychology of Perception*, Nottingham: Skinner.

DOMAN, G. (1965), *Teach your Baby to Read*, London: Jonathan Cape.

DOWNING, J. A. (1963), 'Is a "Mental Age of Six" Essential for "Reading" Readiness?', in *Educational Research 6*, pp. 16-28.

DOWNING, J. A. (1967), *The i. t. a. Symposium*, Slough: N.F.E.R.

EVANS, H. K., *Using Books and Libraries in Primary Schools*, Swansea (50 Sketty Road).

FERNALD, G. M. (1943), *Remedial Techniques in Basic School Subjects*, New York: McGraw Hill.

FERNALD, G. M. and KELLER, H. B. (1921), 'The Effects of Kinaesthetic Factor in Development of Word Recognition', in *Journal of Educational Research, 4*, pp. 355-377.

FISHER, M. (1964), *Intent upon Reading*, Leicester: Brockhampton Press.

FRIES, C. C. (1952), *The Structure of English*, New York: Harcourt, Brace & Co.

FRIES, C. C. (1962), *Linguistics and Reading*, New York: Holt, Rinehart & Winston.

FRIES, C. C., WILSON, R. G. and RUDOLPH, M. K. (1960), *The Merrill Linguistic Readers*, Ohio: Merrill.

GATES, A. I. (1935), *The Improvement of Reading*, New York: Macmillan.

GIBSON, E. J. (1965), 'Learning to Read', in *Science, 148*, pp. 1066.

GIBSON, E. J., OSSER, H. and PICK, A. D. (1963), 'A Study of the Development of Grapheme-phoneme Correspondences', in *Journal of Verbal Learning and Verbal Behaviour, 2*, pp. 142-146.

GIBSON, E. J., PICK, A., OSSER, H. and HAMMOND, M. (1962), 'The Role of Grapheme-phoneme Correspondence in the Perception of Words', in *American Journal of Psychology, 75*, pp. 554-570.

GIONS, J. T. (1958), 'Visual Perceptual Abilities and Early Reading Progress', in *Supplementary Educational Monographs, No 87*.

GOODACRE, E. J. (1967), *Reading in Infant Classes*, Teaching Beginners to Read. Report No 1, Slough: N.F.E.R.

GOODACRE, E. J. (1968), *Teachers and their Pupils' Home Background*. Teaching Beginners to Read. Report No 2, Slough: N.F.E.R.

GOODMAN, K. S. (March 1963), 'A Communicative Theory of the Reading Curriculum', in *Elementary English*.

BIBLIOGRAPHY

HALL, R. A. Jr (1961), *Sound and Spelling in English*, New York: Chilton.

HALL, R. A. Jr (1964), *Introductory Linguistics*, New York: Chilton.

HARRIS, A. J. (1967), 'Psychological Bases of Reading in the U.S.', in Jenkinson, M. D. (ed.), *Reading Instruction: An International Forum*, Newark: I.R.A.

HUEY, J. F. (1966), *Teaching Primary Children*, New York: Holt, Rinehart & Winston.

HUSBAND, R. W. (1928), 'Human Learning on a Four-section Elevated Finger-maze', in *Journal of General Psychology*, *1*, pp. 15-28.

JEFFREY, W. E. and SAMUELS, S. J. (1967), 'Effect of Method of Reading Training on Initial Learning and Transfer', in *Journal of Verbal Learning and Verbal Behaviour*, 6, pp. 354-358.

LEFEVRE, C. A. (1964), *Linguistics and the Teaching of Reading*, New York: McGraw-Hill.

LEVIN, H., BAUN, E., BOSTWICK, S. (1963), in Gibson, E. J., *et al.*, *A Basic Research Programme on Reading*, Project 639. Office of Education, Department of Health Education and Welfare, U.S.A.

LEVIN, H. and WATSON, J. (1963), in Gibson, E. J., *et al.*, *A Basic Research Program on Reading*. Project No. 639. Office of Education, Department of Health, Education and Welfare, U.S.A.

LOVELL, K., BYRNE, C. and RICHARDSON, B. (1963), 'A Further Study of the Long-term Effects of Remedial Teaching', in *British Journal of Educational Psychology*, 33, p. 3

LUNZER, E. A. and MORRIS, J. F. (1968), *Development in Learning*, London: Staples Press.

LYNN, R. (1963), 'Reading Readiness II—Reading Readiness and the Perceptual Abilities of Young Children, in *Educational Research*, 6, pp. 10-15.

MARCHBANKS, G. and LEVIN, H. (1965), 'Cues by which Children Recognize Words', in *Journal of Educational Psychology*, 56, pp. 57-61.

MCCARTHY, D. A. (1956), 'Language Development in Children', in Carmichael, L. (ed.), *Manual of Child Psychology*, New York: Wiley, pp. 492-630.

MCLAUGHLIN, G. H. and COLES, C. R. (1966), 'Efficient Reading 1 and 2', in *New Education*, Work Papers 10 and 11.

MILES, W. (1928), 'The High Relief Finger Maze for Human Learning, in *Journal of General Psychology*, 1, pp. 3-14.

MONROE, M. (1942), *Children Who Cannot Read*, Chicago: University Press.

MONROE, M. and BACKUS, B. (1937), *Remedial Reading*, Boston: Houghton Mifflin.

MORRIS, J. M. (1958), 'Teaching Children to Read—1', in *Educational Research*, 1, pp. 38-49.

MORRIS, J. M. (1959), 'Teaching Children to Read—2', in *Educational Research*, 1, pp. 61-75.

MORRIS, J. M. (1966), *Standards and Progress in Reading*, Slough: N.F.E.R.

MORRIS, R. (1963), *Success and Failure in Learning to Read*, London: Oldbourne.

MURRAY, W. (1964), *The Ladybird Key Words Reading Scheme*, Loughborough: Wills & Hepworth.

NEISSER, U. (June 1964), 'Visual Search', in *Scientific American*. No 486.

O'DONNELL, M. and MUNRO, R. (1961), *The Janet and John Books*, Welwyn: Nisbet.

OBRIST, V. and PICKARD, P. M. (1967), *Time for Reading*, London: Ginn.

PARKER, D. H., *Reading Laboratory Series*, Henley-on-Thames: Science Research Associates.

PLOWDEN *et al.* (1967), *Children and their Primary Schools*, London: H.M.S.O.

POSTMAN, L. and CONGER, B. (1954), 'Verbal Habits and the Visual Recognition of Words', in *Science*, *119*, pp. 671-673.

REID, J. F. (1966), 'Learning to Think about Reading', in *Educational Research*, No 1, pp. 56-62.

REIS, M. (1962), *Fun with Phonics*, Cambridge: Cambridge Art Publishers.

ROBERTS, G. R. (1960), 'A Study of Motivation in Remedial Reading', in *British Journal of Educational Psychology*, *30*, pp. 176-179.

ROBERTS, G. R. (1961), 'An Active Approach to Remedial Reading', in *Forward Trends*, Guild of Teachers of Backward Children.

BIBLIOGRAPHY

ROBERTS, G. R. (14th January 1966), 'Away from the Fun-image of Reading', in *The Teacher*.

ROBERTS, G. R. and LUNZER, E. A. (1968), 'Reading and Learning to Read', in Lunzer, E. A. and Morris, J. F. (eds.), *Development in Learning*, London: Staples Press.

RODNICK, M., STERRITT, G. M. and FLAX, M. (1967), 'Auditory and Visual Rhythm Perception and Reading Ability', in *Child Development*, 38, pp. 581-587.

RUSSELL, D. H. (April 1965), 'Research on the Processes of Thinking with some Applications to Reading', in *Elementary English*, pp. 370-378.

SAMUELS, S. J. (1966), 'Effect of Experimentally Learned Word Associations on the Acquisition of Reading Responses', in *Journal of Educational Psychology*, 57, pp. 159-163.

SAMUELS, S. J. (1967), 'Attentional Process in Reading: the Effect of Pictures on the Acquisition of Reading Responses', in *Journal of Educational Psychology*, 58, pp. 337-342.

SAMUELS, S. J. and JEFFREY, W. E. (1966), 'Discriminability of Words and Letter Cues Used in Learning to Read', in *Journal of Educational Psychology*, 57, pp. 337-340.

SCHONELL, F. J. and SERJEANT, I. (1958), *The Happy Venture Readers*, Edinburgh: Oliver & Boyd.

SCHOOL LIBRARY ASSOCIATION (1966), *Using Books in the Primary School*, S.L.A.

SMITH, N. B. (1966), 'Speed Reading: Benefits and Dangers', in Downing J. (ed.), *The First International Reading Symposium, Oxford, 1964*, London: Cassell.

SOFFIETTI, J. P. (1955), 'Why Children Fail to Read: a Linguistic Analysis', in *Harvard Education Revue*, 35, pp. 63-84.

SOUTHGATE, V. (1963), 'Augmented Roman Alphabet-experiment', in *Educational Review*, 16, No 1, pp. 32-41.

SOUTHGATE, V. and HAVENHAND, J. (1961), *Sounds and Words*, London: University of London Press.

STAUFFER, R. G. (1960), 'Children can Read and Think Critically', in *Education*, 80, pp. 522-525.

STOTT, D. H. (1962), *Programmed Reading Kit*, Glasgow: Holmes.

STOTT, D. H. (1964), *Roads to Literacy*, Glasgow: Holmes.

BIBLIOGRAPHY

TANSLEY, A. E. (1967), *Reading and Remedial Reading*, London: Routledge & Kegan Paul.

TAYLOR, J. and INGLEBY, T. (1966), *Reading with Rhythm*, Set 4, London: Longmans.

THOMAS, O. (1965), *Transformational Grammar and the Teacher of English*, New York: Holt, Rinehart & Winston.

TULVING, E. and GOLD, C. (1963), 'Stimulus Information and Contextual Information as Determinants of Tachistoscopic Recognition of Words', in *Journal of Experimental Psychology*, 63, pp. 319-327.

UNITED KINGDOM READING ASSOCIATION (1967, 1968), *Reading*, Edinburgh: Chambers.

VERNON, M. D. (1957), *Backwardness in Reading*, Cambridge: Cambridge University Press.

VYGOTSKY, L. S. (1962), *Thought and Language*, Cambridge: M.I.T. Press.

WALCUTT, C. C. (1964), *Your Child's Reading*, New York: Cornerstone Library.

WEBB, K. (ed.), Young Puffin and Puffin Books, Harmondsworth: Penguin Books.

WHITEHEAD, A. N. (1962), *The Aims of Education*, London: Benn.